MW01610934

THE POWER OF REINVENTION

ALDO PAPONE

-THE-
POWER
of
REINVENTION

LEADING WITH COURAGE
AND CONVICTION
IN TURBULENT TIMES

For permission please email: paloaltopress@gmail.com

ISBN 978-0-9766512-3-9

Library of Congress Control Number: 2012947134

Printed in the US by Patsons Press, Sunnyvale, CA

First edition published in 2012
Cover and book design by John Seminerio, Artmarks
Proofreading by Charles Garfink

Special discounts on bulk quantities of this book are available
for educational, business or promotional use.

For details please email paloaltopress@gmail.com

PALO

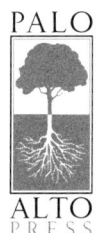

ALTO
PRESS

TO MY WIFE, SANDRA

Thank you for all your support and encouragement,
and for always being there for me.

***

And to my daughter, Renata, and
my grandchildren, Gregory and Alexandra:

This book is for you.

CONTENTS

ACKNOWLEDGEMENTS

As every author knows, writing a book is rarely an individual effort. This one is no exception.

First, I would like to thank Anne Mulcahy for her generous and insightful foreword. If anyone knows the challenges and rewards of reinvention, Anne does. At the helm of Xerox Corporation for a pivotal decade, her decisive and heroic leadership saved one of America's most iconic brands. Anne is a role model for all business leaders tasked with writing a new chapter for their companies.

I am especially fortunate to have been able to reassemble the great team of people who worked with me on my first book, The Power of the Obvious. *I am very proud of the work we have done together over the years. Without them I have no doubt that this project would have taken far longer and been much less enjoyable.*

I would like to thank Kathi Fox for her keen eye and steady hand in guiding my design and production team. My standards are high, and Kathi and her team lived up to them in every respect.

I would also like to thank Susan Thomas. Susan has been my speechwriter for the past seven years, and was instrumental in developing the concepts and content for both of my books. Her counsel, research and writing skills ensured that my vision for this book was superbly translated into reality.

Finally I would like to thank two people who work with me every day at American Express: Dot Miller-Jeffery and Nora Sorrento. Dot knows what it takes to get quality work out the door on time and does so every day with great presence of mind.

I have worked with Nora for 23 years in a most remarkable partnership. She is dedicated, resourceful and completely committed to the company and the work that we do. She shows grace and humor under pressure, and she is not afraid to challenge me when I need it. I am deeply grateful to her for her support and encouragement all these years.

FOREWORD

I have known Aldo since 2000, when I became President and CEO of Xerox. Aldo was a great partner to me navigating first the survival and then the reinvention of Xerox. His timeless wisdom was a source of support and challenge over the years.

Reinvention has never been more important in business. Every company is facing or will face the impact of weakening economies, global forces, technological change and other unanticipated disruptions.

Reinvention is counter to our natural instincts, which is why so many businesses fail to reinvent and become marginalized or irrelevant. When we are confronted with forces of change, it is easy to become entrenched and risk averse. Reinvention is risky and uncomfortable. However, it is the only path to a sustainable future.

Aldo Papone brings his wealth of knowledge and experience to this topic of reinvention. His insights are a great blend of fundamental values and fresh perspectives that propel us toward the future.

Aldo has worked with the best and the brightest over his long business career. His role at American Express was instrumental in keeping this iconic brand in a leadership position over the decades. At Xerox, Aldo helped us navigate a path to strengthen our brand through customer focus and connectivity. I can remember so many times when Aldo would use the voice of the customer to ground our thinking and our actions. His passion for the customer was an inspiration to all of us at Xerox.

In our quest for reinvention, Aldo highlights the need for new perspectives and fresh thinking. He notes that this is an ideal time to be far more inclusive with regard to talent. It is long overdue that we take advantage of the talented women that represent almost half of our workforce and a small fraction of our leadership.

Aldo has a long history of championing and mentoring women leaders—including me! I will always be grateful for his confidence at a time when there were few believers and many skeptics.

This is a timely and insightful book that will help readers embrace the principles of reinvention and shaping the future. I know that Aldo's counsel was instrumental in my journey leading Xerox through a life-threatening crisis to a sustainable and successful future.

I am thrilled that he is sharing his wisdom with a broader audience.

Anne Mulcahy
Former Chairman and CEO, Xerox Corporation
Chairman, Save the Children
New York City
July 2012

INTRODUCTION

It's hard to imagine that seven years have passed since I wrote my first book, *The Power of the Obvious*. It feels like yesterday.

That book was a collection of observations and experiences that shaped my 50-year career in corporate America. It established what I call the Eternal Verities: basic truths that can serve as touchstones for business leaders regardless of industry, what is going on in the world or the pace of change.

Eternal Verity #1: It all comes down to winning. Winning in business is about venturing out into the marketplace and trying to win a customer. That's the only true measure of success or failure in business. And no matter what business you are in, or which company you work for, you must start with the conviction that if someone's going to win, it has to be you.

Eternal Verity #2: Staying at the top takes leadership with staying power. Every business leader faces the challenge of adapting to large currents of change in the world that are largely beyond our control. Leading in times of rapid change is difficult because we can't always see where we're going. That's why enduring leadership is so important: even though our visibility is limited, we must stay focused and on track.

Eternal Verity #3: Relationships matter most of all. Everything comes down to relationships—with your customers, partners, employees, and other stakeholders—but most importantly, with your customers. An important corollary of this truth is that everything you do in the course of contact with a customer either adds to or subtracts from this relationship.

Eternal Verity #4: Brands are a preeminent business asset. Some marketing experts contend that brands are dead and that the trust and value that customers traditionally have placed in brands have no place in today's price-conscious, technology-driven marketplace. I disagree emphatically. If anything is obvious in business it is the lasting power of brands.

In my view, these four Eternal Verities were as relevant when my first book was published in 2005 as they were on my first day of work at my first job in corporate America in 1956.

However, my first book was written just five years into the 21st century. And coming when it did, it was more retrospective than forward looking, more focused on the latter half of the last century than on the inaugural years of the new one. Looking back, the first decade of the 21st century brought dramatic and unprecedented changes to America at home and around the world.

By all measures, it was an astonishing decade because of the magnitude and lasting impact of its main events:

- The tragedy of 9/11 and our heroic recovery in the days and weeks immediately after, which I wrote about at length in *The Power of the Obvious*.

- The Great Recession has had a devastating impact on the American economy—especially jobs—and its global aftermath persists.

- The culture wars of the 1960s and 70s have been reignited and once again threaten to divide our nation along racial, religious and even gender lines.

- Two wars fought in the Middle East simultaneously—one of which is still winding down—have cost America dearly in lost or shattered lives and billions of dollars.

- Innovation in consumer technology has empowered consumers, raising expectations and forever changing how businesses must interact with their customers.

Certainly, these developments have created a seismic shift in the conditions and ground rules for American business that we are just beginning to absorb and understand. In the wake of these extraordinary challenges, some people have asked me:

Are the Eternal Verities still eternal?

Don't the last dozen years prove that sometimes business leaders must fundamentally question all aspects of what it takes to compete and win?

To which I reply, with unwavering conviction: the Eternal Verities are still true. If anything, they are more relevant now than ever—in these times of great change and the uncertainty that comes with the territory.

Why am I so certain?

The Eternal Verities ground us when we can't predict what will happen next, providing comfort in the familiar. Even more importantly, they give us a platform for a way forward—even when we are unsure about the future and progress slows to inches instead of miles a day.

In my view, without the Eternal Verities businesses run the risk of sinking in a quagmire of defeatism. For at times like this, it can feel as if we are being pushed into obsolescence and oblivion. Traffic is roaring up behind us and threatens to knock us out of the fast lane and into the slow lane—and then from the slow lane onto the shoulder of the road—sidelining us forever.

Sometimes when business leaders feel this way, instead of playing to win, they play not to lose. Instead of focusing on the qualities that helped them get where they are today—dynamism, creativity, confidence, enthusiasm— they slide into risk aversion, conservatism, loss of fighting spirit. Instead of feeling youthful and energetic and ready for anything, they feel old and tired and ready to go home.

You get the picture. It's not a pretty one.

Of course, I am exaggerating. But here is my point: at times like this, self-doubt can be our greatest adversary. In the words of the great philosopher, Pogo, "We have met the enemy, and he is us."

So I will tell you this—and I believe it with all my heart: The sky is not falling. The end of the world is not coming. It is not time to give up the fight.

Here is why. With the Eternal Verities at your back, you can re-make yourself. You can re-invent yourself. Chances are you have done it before. Chances are you will do it again.

It is this certainty that led me to the focus of this, my second book: *The Power of Reinvention*.

Now let me say right up front: I am not a big fan of words that begin with the prefix "re-." Even so, you will notice that I used three of them in the last two paragraphs. There are many others I could use:

- Re-think
- Re-evaluate
- Re-engineer
- Re-structure
- Re-focus
- Re-tool
- Re-juvenate
- Re-create

And then there is my all time favorite: Re-architect.

You get my drift.

Throughout my career, I have noticed that words beginning with "re-" seem to emerge and re-emerge (there I go again!) in business conversations during tough times and turmoil. That's because when the ground is shifting beneath us, we wonder if we're doing the right things or doing them in the right ways. It's human nature.

But what is all this "re-" stuff about? Why is it that a prefix that usually means doing something again (repeat, re-do) or going backwards (return, regress) is so often used at precisely the moment we should be going forward?

Over time I have learned that sometimes the place to start on a new path for the future is by thinking about the past.

But let me be clear: I am not hankering for the good old days. Instead, I want to make a case for the good old days of the future, with the past as a foundation.

That's because what is important about the past is the foundation that's been constructed. What will be important in the future is our ability to build on the past in ways that will lead to reinvention.

When I talk about reinvention, I am really talking about growth and renewal. I am talking about staying young.

As a culture, America has a fascination with staying young. When we read about centenarians—people who have reached the age of 100 years or more—we want to know their secrets. We ask, "What keeps you young?"

We listen with rapt attention as they tell us what they eat and drink (no red meat, only red meat—no alcohol, at least two cocktails every day); how much they exercise (twice a day, never); how long they've been married (or how they've avoided it all these years!).

We seek the keys to their longevity so we can unlock it for ourselves.

Sometimes we look for shortcuts. According to The American Society for Aesthetic Plastic Surgery, which has collected plastic surgery procedural statistics since 1997, more than 9 million cosmetic surgical and non-surgical procedures were performed in the United States in 2011—up 197% since statistical tracking began.

Of course, when I talk about staying young, I am not talking about people. And I definitely am not talking about how things look on the surface. I am talking about businesses, which—like people—are living things. And once living things stop growing, they die.

So even though this may sound a little crazy, some of the truths about staying young as people can be applied to staying young as a business:

▶ Goals and dreams keep you young.

▶ Staying competitive keeps you young.

▶ An open mind keeps you young.

▶ Learning new things keeps you young.

▶ Optimism keeps you young.

Sometimes, all of these things together can create a new sense of purpose. And then suddenly, you have renewal—and you're young again.

I've watched the parade for a long time. I try to do these things every day. I can tell you it really works.

But the analogy between business and the human body starts to break down quickly. That's because unfortunately, the biology of human aging is much more difficult to reverse than the lifecycles of business. For example, it is unlikely that even with great effort and enthusiasm I will win a gold medal in the high hurdles at the Olympics.

But unlike a human being, a business can be renewed again and again indefinitely. For examples we need look no further than two companies I admire: American Express and Apple.

I admit I may be biased, but I believe American Express is one of the best examples anywhere of a company that continually reinvents itself.

Formed in 1850 by the merger of two competing express companies, American Express specialized in shipping packages smaller than the bulk freight railroads handled but larger than the U.S. Postal Service size limits. The company also carried packages that required special handling or were particularly valuable.

From humble beginnings, American Express has become a global financial services company, the world's largest travel business and one of the most trusted and valuable brands in the world.

You can be sure it hasn't done any of that by standing still. And I am on solid ground when I say that despite the many changes at American Express since it was founded more than a century and a half ago, the company could still be considered a work in progress. It always will be— and that is the way it should be.

Then, consider Apple. With innovation, design and simplicity as its core brand values, Apple has revolutionized three industries so far: personal computing, music and mobile phones. With the growing popularity of the iPad, the company is well on its way to inventing a fourth industry.

Along the way it recast itself from a niche computing company to a consumer technology powerhouse.

The capacity to reinvent itself—bringing along with it entire ecosystems of companies and industries—explains why on any given day, depending on the vagaries of the public markets, Apple is the most valuable company in the world.

American Express and Apple are living proof that instead of feeling stymied or boxed in by the present state of things—whatever they might be—we should feel optimistic. In a grow-or-die world, we can choose to grow and thrive.

That in a nutshell is what "re-" words are all about. They simply invite us to take a fresh look at our companies and the world around us.

And that is exactly what I am encouraging you to do as you read this book.

As was the case when I wrote my first book, a disclaimer is in order. *The Power of Reinvention* is not a manifesto for how to reinvent your company. It does not contain everything you need to know.

Instead, it is my own personal view of key topics and essential questions you could ask and answer to spark growth and renewal in your company. The topics are evergreen: leadership, talent and the role of brands. But they deserve a fresh look. The questions are specific to these changing times:

Has the Great Recession reset the American economy for good? What is the task of leadership in a world transformed?

Why are there still so few women in leadership positions in business? Is it time for U.S. corporations to make the decision to rise above the statistics?

What can businesses gain by hiring veterans returning from Iraq and Afghanistan? Can we tap into new military leadership and work styles—developed during two wars unlike any others we have experienced—to solve the business challenges we face today?

What do Millennials need and want to be successful? How must leadership and working styles change as our next-generation leaders enter the workforce and assume positions of responsibility?

How has digital technology changed consumer expectations? What is the new consumer journey and where do brands fit in?

Now as you know, visualizing a new future can be energizing. But it can also be challenging…and sometimes even uncomfortable. To that, all I can I say is that in my experience a little discomfort can be a good thing.

There is an urban legend—an instructive story thought to be true, although it is not true—about a biology experiment involving a frog. Perhaps you've heard it.

The story goes that you can place a frog in cold water and then raise the temperature so slowly that the frog is boiled before he knows what is happening.

Not surprisingly, this story is used as a cautionary tale about how important it is for businesses to act swiftly and decisively—preferably before something catastrophic happens.

Well it turns out that if you actually do this to a frog—which I am certainly not recommending—instead of being lulled into complacency, he will become more active as the water heats up. And assuming the container has a hole large enough, the frog will leap out long before he is boiled.

The fact that the frog in boiling water story is not true does not diminish the value of its real metaphor, which is the frog's ability to escape.

The frog is certainly motivated to escape. Being in hot water will do that. But if he cannot find a way out of his situation—and fast—his fate is a foregone conclusion.

I would suggest to you that reinvention—like the frog's escape—requires three things: motivation, a way out and a sense of urgency.

In that spirit, I hope you find this book a little bit like a pot of boiling water.

LEADERSHIP
IN THE NEW NORMAL

Has the Great Recession reset the American economy for good?

What is the task of leadership
in a world transformed?

After nearly five years of global economic turmoil—the likes of which we have not seen since before World War II—in my view we are entering a post-crisis era.

Notice I did not say we are out of the woods. As I write this in July 2012, the unemployment rate is stuck at 8.2%, economic growth in the United States and China is slowing, and the European financial crisis threatens the future of the eurozone. This is not the first time in this start-and-stop recovery that things look a little worse after having looked a little better. It may not be the last.

Pessimists argue that the world financial situation remains unstable and that an economic jolt anywhere in the world could trigger another sharp economic decline. Optimists say fears of another recession are greatly exaggerated.

I don't know who is correct—the pessimists or the optimists. But as a businessman and a pragmatist, I'm sure of three things.

- Today's business climate is uncertain and extraordinarily fast changing.

- So many market conditions have changed at once that we are facing a set of circumstances different from anything we've seen in the past.

● Current challenges will persist for another three, four or perhaps even five years—so we'd better get used to what some observers are calling "the new normal."

McKinsey & Company was among the first to apply the term, "the new normal," to our current state. In March 2009, McKinsey's Worldwide Managing Director Ian Davis (now retired from the firm) wrote, "It is increasingly clear that the current downturn is fundamentally different from recessions of recent decades. We are experiencing not merely another turn of the business cycle, but a restructuring of the economic order."

Seven months later, in December 2009, the firm assembled a roundtable of chief strategy officers to ponder the question of how to navigate in this new normal: a world of shrinking planning cycles, growth paths that had become increasingly hard to predict, and business assumptions that once seemed indisputable now in question.

While economists and academics will debate these conclusions for years to come, my interest lies more in what such extraordinary times demand of companies and their leaders. It surely isn't business as usual. And while the future is inherently unknowable, the level of uncertainty today has shaken the confidence of American business leaders as no other economic downturn in my 50 years in corporate America.

Are U.S. companies stronger for the recession?

Not all the economic news is doom and gloom. A recent analysis of corporate financial reports by the *Wall Street Journal* showed that the sales, profits and employment in 2011 of members of Standard & Poor's 500 stock index exceeded the totals of 2007, before the financial crisis began. The takeaway is that large American companies have emerged from the recession "more productive, more profitable, flush with cash and less burdened by debt."

How can that be? Clearly, some companies used the recession to take a close look at expenses and found ways to cut costs, starting with eliminating jobs. By late spring of 2012, the United States economy was producing more goods and services than it did when the recession officially began in December 2007—but with about five million fewer workers.

Despite these productivity gains, a slow-growing economy may mean that a real recovery—the kind that produces jobs as well as profits and top line growth—

may prove elusive. That's because cost cutting alone is not enough. Recent research from Harvard Business School showed that companies that simply cut costs faster and deeper than their competitors during a recession don't necessarily flourish once the recession is over.

The Harvard research analyzed the actions of 4,700 companies over the three global recessions prior to the current one—the recessions of 1980-82, 1990-91 and 2000-02, respectively—and correlated these actions to the companies' success before and after. The conclusion was companies that balance cutting costs to survive with investing in the future are the ones that do well after a recession is over.

In other words, companies with leaders who think beyond the moment and act boldly for the future during a downturn are much more likely to emerge strong and prepared to win when it's over.

I have lived through many economic downturns and financial crises of one type or another in my career, several of which caused prolonged and exhausting periods of uncertainty. If there is one thing I have learned about times like these, it is that leaders must not panic. Panic leads to paralysis—an unwillingness to do anything risky—and sometimes an inability to do anything at all!

This is exactly the opposite of what is required during times like these. Great leaders have proven time and time again that flexibility and adaptability are always the solution.

And when the future is especially uncertain, great leaders have also proven that instead of taking a risk-averse course of action, success lies in bold moves that look beyond today's crisis to new strength and leadership in the future.

That, of course, is called reinvention.

Reinvention as a way forward

Reinvention is the theme of this book, but I know that reinvention has become something of a buzzword. From business books to workshops to high-priced consultants, everyone has an opinion about how to drive and manage change in an organization at scale.

Now in theory and on paper, reinvention is an appealing concept. But in reality, people and companies are filled with old cultural norms. And reinvention—like oil on water—can rest comfortably on the surface of an organization for a very long time.

You might argue that companies, by definition, change continuously in reaction to developments internally and in the market. And they do. But sometimes a company must change more quickly than is allowed by a gradual evolution. Sometimes companies need to break from the past and do so at an accelerated pace of change.

One dictionary definition of reinvention is "to invent again or anew." Another is "to remake or makeover, as in a different form."

Both are good definitions for what companies must sometimes do to thrive in the face of change. But they can sound scary because they suggest that you must leave your comfort zone and fly headlong into unknown territory.

But the truth is we're all old hands at reinvention.

Think back to your childhood. I am sure that all of us spent time as children dreaming of becoming actors, authors, explorers and other glamorous and exciting professions. Somewhere along the way, we changed from being dreamy youngsters and started to focus on our adult priorities. That is why we are all doing what we do today—and not scaling Mount Everest. (Unless of course, you actually are scaling Mount Everest!)

The reinvention you and I underwent in moving from childhood to adulthood is not unlike the changes that businesses experience. Businesses are a collection of like-minded people who work together toward a common goal. To be successful over time, businesses must change—and sometimes energetically, as in times of crisis.

Consider Apple. On the brink of bankruptcy in 1997, co-founder Steve Jobs returned to the company as CEO and immediately began introducing new computer and software products. Meanwhile, Jobs charged Apple's engineers with developing a product unlike anything Apple or anyone else had ever produced before.

That product, the iPod, was introduced in 2001 and today holds more than 70% of the worldwide market for portable music players. It was the driving force behind Apple's cultural and financial reinvention—by all measures an extreme makeover—from a marginalized computer manufacturer to a 21st century consumer electronics leader. And it was just the beginning.

In 2003, Apple launched iTunes, a music distribution service that has since expanded to include movies, television shows, free education content from the world's most prestigious educational institutions, and applications for mobile devices.

Then in 2007 Apple launched the iPhone, powered by its new mobile platform iOS, and in 2010, the iPad. iOS now powers the iPod touch, iPhone and iPad—together the best selling mobile products on the planet—and arguably the foundation of Apple's future.

The abrupt jumps Apple has made from one product (computers) to another (portable music players) to another (mobile phones) are not unlike many of the transitions American Express has made since it was founded in 1850.

As you know, while all reinventions involve a break from the past, not all are quite so dramatic as those made by Apple. Instead, some are based on taking advantage of adjacent opportunities in which elements of existing products or channels are leveraged in a way that responds to consumer and marketplace needs.

American Express is an example of a company that has continually reinvented itself by embracing adjacent opportunities. Some examples:

1882—American Express built on its reputation as a reliable and secure delivery service for bank documents such as checks and interbank transfers to provide the first non–alterable money order.

1891—American Express introduced the Traveler's Cheque.

1915—American Express opened a travel division.

1959—American Express released the first-ever widely used plastic charge card.

1983—American Express brought together its business travel and corporate card businesses to create a new business model combining business travel and card payment data for corporations.

1995—American Express launched Membership Rewards, a terrific program reflecting a major change within the company.

1999—American Express released its first credit card (as opposed to charge card) called Blue—considered the nation's first "smart" card because it contained a chip on which a customer's credit and debit information could be stored.

2011—American Express unveiled Serve, a reloadable prepaid account whose funds can be accessed electronically from any device with a browser and an Internet connection, including smartphones.

Another type of reinvention occurs when an organization sets out in new directions to expand its offerings, making it more relevant to more people. One example of such an organization is the Hospital for Special Surgery (HSS) in New York City.

I've been closely associated with HSS for the past 30 years, first as a patient, then a member of the Board of Trustees and since 1998, Co-Chair of the Board of Trustees. Founded in 1863, HSS today is the leading hospital for orthopedics in United States. But it hasn't always held that distinction.

HSS' initial focus was on helping children with physical disabilities. Over the years, the hospital adapted to changing demand, for example, by providing orthopedic care for returning veterans from both world wars and starting in the 1920s becoming a leader in post-polio care and rehabilitation. Today children and adults come to the hospital from around the world to receive treatment for orthopedic conditions and injuries, and autoimmune diseases. HSS is also the official hospital for major New York area professional sports teams and routinely treats other elite athletes from around the world.

Importantly, while HSS has never strayed from its original mission—high-quality patient care, research and education focused exclusively on orthopedics and rheumatology—the hospital has demonstrated a remarkable ability to grow and expand profitability. This type of continual renewal and reinvention is no less difficult and important to achieve than dramatic reinventions necessitated by disruptions in the market that threaten an organization's survival.

In addition to their differences, there are several things that Apple, American Express, the Hospital for Special Surgery and others that are masters of reinvention have in common. One of them is they have strong leaders who recognize when business as usual will not suffice and instead take bold moves to create new futures for their companies.

Of course Steve Jobs was such a leader. He is rightly credited with revolutionizing five industries in his lifetime—personal computers, music, mobile phones and mobile computing while at Apple, and as the head of Pixar, animated feature films. Pixar is the studio that brought us movies such as *Toy Story*, *A Bug's Life* and *Finding Nemo* during Jobs' tenure as CEO. The studio is now part of Disney.

Jobs died in October 2011, but I have no doubt that had he lived he would have continued to disrupt entire industries for many years to come.

American Express has had its share of bold leaders, starting with J.C. Fargo, who was President of the company in the 1890s. After returning home from a lengthy tour of Europe—where he was frustrated by the time-consuming process of presenting Letters of Credit to banks in order to obtain cash in local currencies—he directed his staff to create a payment product that could be exchanged easily, on the spot and on sight.

The solution was the Traveler's Cheque, a revolutionary product so simple and perfectly conceived that it's been modified only slightly over the years. As the 19th century ended, the Traveler's Cheque was the main vehicle of American Express' growth.

Another American Express leader of Fargo's caliber is our current Chairman and CEO Ken Chenault. More than once in his 31 years with the company—11 years as CEO—Ken has made bold decisions that have taken the company in new directions.

Hired into American Express by Lou Gerstner in 1981, Ken's first assignment was to lead the company's underperforming merchandise services business.

The business sold luxury items to American Express Cardmembers via direct marketing. In just two years Ken was able to double sales by matching marketing offers with Cardmembers' interests.

Ken's next assignment was to lead the company's card business, where he pushed to broaden the portfolio— a continuation of the strategy he followed in turning around merchandise services, which was to segment customers and develop different products to meet their needs. There were those who questioned the wisdom of expanding the company's card offerings in this way, believing that it would drag down the image and prestige of the brand. Ken persevered and proved his critics wrong.

Another example of Ken's new vision for the company was his introduction of the American Express Membership Rewards program. Today one of the most popular and successful initiatives of its kind in any industry, at the time of its introduction the program was resisted by internal skeptics who felt it would sully the brand. In truth it had the opposite effect and has enhanced the brand and its value to our Cardmembers.

Ken was named CEO of American Express in January 2001, and just nine months later was thrust into the tragedy of 9/11. With company headquarters located right next to the World Trade Center, American Express lost 11 employees that day. Ken's leadership during that time was a perfect combination of steady and heroic, courageous and compassionate. Largely because of his leadership, American Express was able to get back into the full swing of business in short order.

Ken's leadership was tested again during the recent economic downturn. American Express remained profitable each quarter while many of its competitors did not; merchant and Cardmember retention rates were stable; and despite the slowdown, Ken insisted that the company continue to invest in the business. These actions enabled the company to emerge from the most acute phase of the crisis stronger than ever.

As a result of Ken's leadership both during severe business challenges and business as usual, the company is today the world's leader in charge and credit cards, the world's largest travel agency and one of the world's most respected brands.

What is most notable about the leadership story at the Hospital for Special Surgery is the organization's long history of creating collaborative leadership teams that carefully and respectfully balance medical priorities with business imperatives.

The challenge is that sometimes when a physician is at the helm of a medical institution the organization sacrifices financial health and well being for patient care. Conversely, when a businessperson is in charge, sometimes dollars and cents are emphasized over patient care and medical outcomes. Both, of course, are absolutely necessary for hospitals to thrive—and to become leaders in their areas of specialty or communities.

I am proud to be associated with a medical organization that has cracked the code on how to blend medical and business priorities to create a world-class healthcare institution that is also financially sound. Much of the credit for the accomplishments of the Hospital for Special Surgery over the past five years goes to its current leadership team: President and CEO Lou Shapiro; Surgeon-in-Chief and Medical Director Tom Sculco; Physician-in-Chief and Chair of the Division of Rheumatology Mary Crow; Chief Scientific Officer Steve Goldring; and my fellow Co-Chair Dean O'Hare.

What does leadership look like in the new normal?

If you read my first book, *The Power of the Obvious,* you know that leadership is a topic I've spent a great deal of time thinking about in my career.

Leadership means different things to different people in different contexts. I believe, for example, that there are enduring qualities of great leaders…and that there are attributes of great leaders that change with the times.

These variations sometimes make it difficult for us to get our arms around leadership. Some would even argue that leadership is a "black box" art—we can see the outside of it, but we have no idea how it works.

I respectfully disagree. It is never easy, but it is possible to develop models of leadership that can be applied in specific organizations at specific times. In fact, it is crucial that we do so because only organizations that study leadership, demystify it, model it and connect its models to concrete behaviors will be successful growing and developing its leaders.

A lifetime of observing leadership in all conditions has led me to the conclusion that there are several common denominators of leaders who have successfully reinvented their businesses. They are worth examining as we consider leadership in the new normal.

First, leaders who have led their organizations through a reinvention are able to visualize a future far greater than anyone thought possible. While others are complaining that they cannot see far enough ahead to make good decisions about the future, reinvention masters pierce the fog of uncertainty and think about how to position the company once the crisis has passed and things return to normal. They do this even at times when no one seems to know how long the crisis will last and what normal will be like on the other side.

Second, and equally important, they do logical things to make it happen. They have a plan—because vision alone is not a plan—and they adapt it as needed. They add and subtract, revise and rework. They eliminate distractions. They build momentum.

Third, leaders at the helm as a company reinvents itself ensure that no matter how environmental conditions are changing, the company holds to a steady pace of progress.

Now my last point might seem like a contradiction to the need for adaptability, but it isn't really. It's an elegant yet powerful idea—that steady progress in the middle of chaos is essential to success.

It was beautifully explored in the latest book by Jim Collins, *Great by Choice,* co-authored by Morten Hansen. Collins is the author of the modern business classics *Good to Great* and *Built to Last*.

For me the most compelling concept in the book is the 20-Mile March, a term the authors used to illustrate this need to move ahead at a steady rate no matter what. To bring the concept to life, they described a famous race that took place from 1910 to 1912 between two teams determined to be the first one in modern history to reach the South Pole. Robert Falcon Scott of England led one team and Norwegian Roald Amundsen led the other.

Both men were about the same age and had the same expertise. Their teams were similarly outfitted and they started their 1,400 mile journeys at the same time. However, the outcomes were tragically different. On December 14, 1911, Amundsen reached the South Pole first, and then returned himself and his team safely to their home base. Scott and his team reached the South Pole five weeks later, saw that they had failed in their quest, and turned around to return to their base. All perished on the return trip.

Despite the similarities between the two teams, there were important differences. Amundsen used dogs to pull sledges filled with supplies while he and his men expertly skied alongside. Scott first tried using ponies to pull the sledges, but when that failed—ponies were not well suited to the climate or terrain—he and his men pulled the sledges themselves.

But what really made the difference for Amundsen was his insistence that no matter what the weather conditions, the team would try to march 20 miles every day. This required extraordinary discipline when the weather was good—even when the men felt like continuing they stopped to rest after 20 miles. When the weather was bad and progress was difficult, marching 20 miles required superhuman grit.

In contrast, Scott had no such regimen, and instead just responded to the weather. When the weather was good, he would sometimes drive his team to exhaustion by traveling as far as they could. When the weather was bad, he would often sit in his tent and lament his bad luck.

The story is meant to convey that the 20-Mile March is more than a philosophy; it's about putting in place simple, concrete and realistic performance goals, and then rigorously pursuing them to stay on track.

In creating new futures for their companies, leaders do all of these things because the future never just happens—it's made. Sometimes it's made by accident, but more often by people acting consciously and seizing opportunities. And that can only occur not when people resist change, but when they welcome and manage it.

The good news is that the art of reinvention can be learned. The trick for leaders is to help the people who work for them discover a new reality that changes the way they perceive and experience the company…and then give them the flexibility and authority to implement this reality.

The value of storytelling

One way to do this is to describe the future as a story—a screenplay for the drama about to unfold. From the first Greek tragedy to daily newspapers to CNN, the main vehicle used to shape opinion—and change behavior—is the story. As Aristotle figured out more than 2,000 years ago, stories—and especially simple stories—work quite well.

Henry Ford knew this when he developed a compelling vision for his new automobile company, which he founded at a time when only the very rich could afford cars.

Ford said: "It's time to democratize the automobile. I will build a motor car for the great multitude…so low in price that no man making a good salary will be unable to own one…and enjoy with his family the blessing of hours of pleasure in God's open spaces… The horse will have disappeared from our highways, the automobile will be taken for granted."

We are all well aware of how Ford's vision of the future transformed not just his young company, but an entire industry.

So what are the essential elements of a good business reinvention story?

First, it must answer the questions: why does the company need this reinvention? Is it because external factors—such as our current global financial crisis—have changed the rules of the game? Or has the competition become more powerful? Or is technology forcing an overhaul of time-honored business processes?

It's important that the story go beyond the superficial to why these things need to happen. This requires brutal honesty, which is difficult and rare because it can call into question the company's previous decisions and its current leaders.

I once read a fascinating story about Chiyoshi Misawa, founder and president of Misawa Homes, at one time the largest homebuilder in Japan. To stop the momentum of out-of-date assumptions and policies, Mr. Misawa would "die" about once a decade. He would send a memo to his company formally announcing "the death of your president."

Then, when employees resisted change because they were used to the old way of doing things, Mr. Misawa would declare: "That was the way things were done under Mr. Misawa. He is dead. Now, how shall we proceed?"

This was his way of forcing the whole company to periodically rethink everything—free from the concern of offending their leader.

The second question a business reinvention story must answer is: where is the company heading?

This requires true creativity—to paint a picture of the future and make it so convincing that people can make it happen. It also requires something genuinely new—not just doing something better or faster or cheaper—but something different. Ideas that drive reinvention almost always move beyond something others already know.

The third question a good story must answer is: how can we reach our goal?

This is more practical and includes details such as tasks, phases, timing and responsibilities.

But these details alone are not sufficient. A sense of the personal responsibility that everyone must feel—as well as the personal experience everyone will have once the future is achieved—must infuse the story so that it becomes real.

This is important because emotions play a leading role in business reinventions. Even senior executives fall victim to emotions such as fear and denial in conditions such as those we face today.

My friend and colleague Shelly Lazarus, retired Chairman of American Express' longtime advertising agency Ogilvy & Mather, once told me a memorable story about one leader's technique for managing emotions in tough conditions. She heard it from a man who for many years had commanded a submarine for the British Navy, leading 100 men who were kept below surface for weeks and months at a time.

It sounds so simple, but was very effective. This submarine commander would invite all of the officers under his command to his cabin every evening at 6:00 p.m. for a glass of wine. The gathering was informal, and the naval commander just let the men talk and blow off steam.

These breaks from the constant stress of their daily lives undersea in close quarters helped the officers rejuvenate to face another day.

Different techniques will work for different organizations. But it is up to CEOs to help their leaders work through the powerful emotions involved in reinvention and managing change.

The power of many trumps the power of one

So far, I have talked about the insight and impact that any leader at the top of an organization that is reinventing itself must have. And while there will always be standout leaders—people who are able to get others in their organization to believe and to follow—the role of the individual leader has changed. There's just too much for one man or woman to know or do for a one-person show. Instead, we need people at all levels with different sets of skills, all of exceptional quality.

In fact, in my view, no company can succeed at reinvention with a tiny percentage of its people exerting leadership. Instead, we need many people who are stimulated to act on their own initiative and take responsibility.

But when I say, "act on their own initiative" and "take responsibility," I mean that people must do these things but they must do so within the team. That is the only way an organization can be successful at reinvention—through teams that share a common vision and common goals, yet are nimble, resilient and can capitalize on the unexpected.

So another common denominator of leaders who have successfully reinvented their businesses is this: they build strong teams—teams that leverage the strengths, weaknesses and motivations of each team member. They encourage constructive debate to generate options and gain buy-in. And they create a safe environment for risk taking by team members.

Even Steve Jobs—a notorious lone wolf—brought other great leaders into Apple's leadership team. One of them was Tim Cook, the operational wizard who helped Steve Jobs realize his vision and who succeeded him as CEO. Another was Jonathan Ive, the brilliant designer and holder of more than 600 patents who gave physical form to Jobs' pet projects, starting with the iPod.

The power of the team is a classic example of something whose merits are so obvious that we don't think about it enough. And that's a mistake. Really, we should think about teamwork every day, because it never fails to produce rich rewards. And in times like these, it is more important to share knowledge and good ideas so they can be rapidly duplicated and implemented by others.

Having said that teamwork is indispensable, I also want to say that the power of individuals—their unique qualities and experiences—is equally critical. The appreciation and enhancing of diversity of approach and perspectives on how to achieve success are to me a key attribute of companies that emerge stronger than ever from periods of economic turmoil and slow growth.

To this point, let me mention—and contrast—two great athletes.

Both are individual superstars, but both have very different perspectives—the point being that it's not necessary or even desirable for everyone on the team to bring the same practices and approaches to the table.

The first—and more famous—is Michael Phelps, the phenomenal American swimmer. Prior to the 2012 Summer Olympics in London, Phelps had already won 16 Olympic medals in his career: six gold and two bronze in Athens in 2004 and eight gold in Beijing in 2008.

While no one expected a repeat of his performance in Beijing—including Phelps himself—no one had any doubt he would bring home additional medals. He did, and with 22 medals Phelps now holds the record for the most Olympic medals in history.

Phelps has astonishing natural gifts that are ideal for swimming—he is 6' 4" tall yet weighs just 165 pounds, has a long, thin torso, a disproportionate arm span, size 14 feet, and hyper-mobile ankles. But it is his training regimen that is the stuff of legends.

Phelps has trained with Bob Bowman, Head Coach and CEO of the North Baltimore Aquatic Club—near where Phelps grew up—since he was 11 years old. At times Phelps has said that Bowman reminds him of a drill sergeant because of his focused and disciplined approach to training.

Colorful adjectives Phelps has used to describe his coach include "intense" and "insane."

Bowman is the mastermind behind the game plan for Michael Phelps' unparalleled success as an athlete. But Phelps has embraced and executed it flawlessly.

It begins with stroke mechanics, which Bowman and Phelps have endlessly analyzed and optimized to near perfection. And then there are the workouts: stretching, warm ups, more warm ups, swimming, lactose testing (to make sure all Phelps' muscles are functioning properly), massages, naps—and all of these training elements every day, more often twice a day, for a total of six hours.

All of this activity is fueled by a daily intake of 12,000 calories: fried egg sandwiches, omelets, grits, French toast, pancakes, pasta, ham and cheese sandwiches, more pasta, pizza—washed down by energy drinks.

At night, Phelps sleeps in a high-altitude chamber, which—by creating a low-oxygen environment—forces Phelps to exercise his lungs even while sleeping.

Now, contrast Phelps with Araceli Segarra, the first Spanish women to successfully climb Mount Everest. Segarra is a great climber and leader of climbing expeditions. Since 1991 she's climbed almost every famous peak—from Nepal, Tibet and Pakistan to Kenya, Morocco, Argentina and Canada. She was featured in two IMAX movies about climbing, *Everest* and *Return to Everest*.

When Segarra talks about her sport, she's the absolute opposite of Michael Phelps. She doesn't obsess with climbing mechanics, arcane technical skills or the minute details of training.

In fact, she says her greatest preparation is in packing her equipment. "It takes me two days to pack my two carrying bags," she has said.

What about her training program? "I climb. I love to climb," she has said.

How did she overcome the freezing temperatures on Mount Everest? "I got in a sleeping bag with my two climbing partners. The secret is to keep warm."

To her, climbing is about passion and love for the sport—she's not fixated on the details. To Michael Phelps and Bob Bowman, the details are everything.

Totally different approaches—and both are champions.

Now I suspect that Segarra's preparation is just as good as Phelps' and Phelps' love and passion for the sport are just as great as Segarra's. But they go about it in diametrically different ways.

Phelps has his ways…two workouts a day, 12,000 calories, sleeping in a high-altitude chamber. Segarra has her instinctive feel for a situation. Phelps measures the lactose in his muscles. Segarra takes the measure of the mountain…and instinctively understands the actions that will deliver success.

If there is a lesson here for all business leaders, it is that there are many approaches, many cultures, many beliefs and we should look for them, appreciate them and encourage them. Especially as we seek answers to some of the most difficult challenges we've ever faced.

Failure as a prelude to success

I want to mention one more common denominator of leaders who have led their companies to reinvent themselves. That is a forgiveness of failure.

Now to be clear: I don't mean forgiveness of incompetence, carelessness or recklessness. And I don't mean forgiveness of individuals who fail time and again and never learn anything from their mistakes. I mean forgiveness of risk takers whose decisions or actions might sometimes miss the mark.

This type of forgiveness is essential because failure is a fact of life. It's a law of nature. It is inevitable.

And make no mistake about it. Anyone who dares to do something different…something important…something bold…is going to fail at some part of the process.

In fact, failure is part of the process—maybe even the most important part.

History is full of famous failures:

- Thomas Edison tried more than 9,000 designs for the light bulb before getting it right.

- Henry Ford lost all the money from his first group of investors without producing a single car.

- Walt Disney was fired from his job as a newspaper reporter by an editor who told him he "lacked imagination and had no original ideas."

- Michael Jordan was cut from his high school basketball team.

What does this mean for leaders of companies reinventing themselves in the new normal?

- Your goal is not to not lose. Your goal is to win. And as we all know, the team that plays defensively —not to lose—almost never wins.

- You must be agile. The world changes every day. Be prepared for that. And if you sense failure on your current course, rethink and restart.

- Never give up. Your job is to take risks and build something great.

That's what reinvention is all about.

So in the new normal—whatever it might be—go out and imagine new ways in which your company can serve its customers; new approaches to strategy and planning; and new markets and new opportunities that might serve as growth engines for the future.

And then go out and build a strong team that can make it so.

TALENT
IN THE 21ST CENTURY

Why are there still so few women in leadership positions in business?

Is it time for U.S. corporations to make the
decision to rise above the statistics?

My first job in corporate America was at Macy's, one of the country's premier retailers. I worked in the company's flagship store at Herald Square at Broadway and 34th Street in New York City, which is still billed as the "World's Largest Store." The year was 1956 and my job was an entry-level position in store management.

I thoroughly enjoyed store management, but after several years I made a lateral move within Macy's to become an assistant buyer for children's wear. While it's common in retail to rise through the ranks through one of two paths—either store management or buying—it's the rare retail executive who has substantial experience on both paths. I wanted to be one of them.

Readers of my first book will recall that as an assistant buyer for children's wear at Macy's, I worked for a woman with the memorable name of Gladys Goldfinger. Mrs. Goldfinger was Macy's head buyer for children's wear and as such, she always had several assistant buyers working for her. We all shared a 10 x 12 office in a corner of the 4th floor children's department. My desk sat adjacent to hers.

Mrs. Goldfinger was so respected for her buying acumen and experience that many of the phone calls she received were from others at Macy's asking for her opinion. Because of the proximity of my desk to hers, I could not help overhearing many of her conversations. A frequent caller was Ted Ronick, President of Product Development at Macy's. From his lofty position, even Ted sought out Mrs. Goldfinger for advice—and for good reason.

By all measures, Mrs. Goldfinger was an excellent buyer. But she also was a superb supervisor and mentor—one of the best developers of young talent I have ever known. It was from her that I learned one of the most important lessons of my career: understanding the customer requires firsthand knowledge and attention to detail for which there is no substitute.

Even then, in the late 1950s, buyers at Macy's had sophisticated and complete management reports to help us understand what merchandise was selling and what wasn't. Still, Mrs. Goldfinger required all of her assistant buyers to adopt a practice that she herself followed faithfully. Instead of taking the elevator closest to our offices to and from lunch every day, Mrs. Goldfinger insisted that we walk through the floor.

Our assignment was to observe what people were buying that day, talk to customers and get their reactions to the merchandise and the experience of shopping at Macy's. We had to report back to Mrs. Goldfinger every day about our observations—and we faced a barrage of questions if she deemed our accounts superficial or lacking in depth.

As Mrs. Goldfinger would say, "To be successful in retail, you've got to get into the customer's head."

What Mrs. Goldfinger demanded certainly made us much more effective and timely in children's wear buying decisions. It also showed us that while detailed sales reports and research generated by others are valuable, nothing could replace your own personal knowledge of customer buying behaviors and satisfaction levels.

This lesson served me well throughout my career at Macy's, where ultimately I became Senior Vice President of Merchandising. It also made a huge difference in 1974, when I was hired away from Macy's by American Express CEO Jim Robinson to be President of American Express' Travel Division.

As you might imagine, after 18 years at Macy's I knew retail. But I did not know travel. In fact, the day I took over at American Express Travel was my first day in the travel business.

Why was I hired instead of a travel industry veteran? Because I brought something to my new job at American Express that was then relatively rare for a senior executive: intimate familiarity with consumers and a deep understanding of consumer needs.

Jim Robinson recognized the value of that experience, and that is why he hired me. Mrs. Goldfinger certainly understood its value. Lucky for me, I worked for her at a formative time in my career.

She could have done more

I would like to say I fully appreciated Mrs. Goldfinger when I was working for her. But as a young man in my 20s, I did not. That took a few years.

It took a few more years for me to recognize the magnitude of the contribution Mrs. Goldfinger was making to Macy's. She trained dozens of assistant buyers over the years in techniques for "getting inside the heads of consumers." She also demanded that we apply the insights we gleaned when making our buying decisions. Many of Mrs. Goldfinger's assistant buyers—including me—used these skills to rise up the ladder and serve in important jobs for Macy's.

I'm embarrassed to say it took me a few years longer

to realize something else. Back then Mrs. Goldfinger was laying the groundwork for dozens of primarily young men to achieve leadership positions at Macy's that she herself had little hope of attaining—because of her gender.

I cannot help wondering now what kind of career Mrs. Goldfinger would have had if she had been born a few decades later. She was a unique woman and she could have done more.

But Mrs. Goldfinger also was a product of her time. In the late 50s, cultural notions about women's appropriate role in society dictated the limits of her role in business—and perhaps even created limits in her own mind. I'll never know.

The war opens doors for working women

What I do know is that World War II created opportunities for American women to work outside the home. More than 16 million men from 18 to 45 years old either enlisted or were drafted into the military, and many were shipped overseas to serve. Their absence, combined with the demands of wartime, created a need for workers so great that millions of women, students and even retired people entered the labor force.

When the war ended, factories closed, causing some women to lose their jobs. Returning veterans replaced others. But most women who wanted to continue working did so.

For a long time though, working women were confined to supporting or helping professions. They worked as nurses, teachers, secretaries, sales clerks or— as in the case of Mrs. Goldfinger—department supervisors in retail stores. This situation did not change much until the women's movement of the 1960s and 70s, when women made enormous social gains. Not only did the number of working women grow dramatically, the type of work women were doing expanded to include jobs and professions traditionally considered "men's work": law, medicine, science and technology, and business management.

By most relevant measures, the last half a century has been a time of revolutionary change for working women. According to U.S. Department of Labor and U.S. Census Bureau statistics:

● Women make up nearly 47% of the total U.S. workforce.

- Women hold more than half of the jobs in high-paying management, professional and related occupations.

- 37% of employed women have college degrees compared to 30% of employed men.

- 56% of students enrolled in college are women.

Are we there yet?

Based on these statistics, you might think that women have made similar gains in achieving leadership positions in business. Sadly that is not the case.

According to Catalyst, a leading nonprofit organization expanding opportunities for women in business, today women are just:

- 3.6% of Fortune 500 CEOs;

- 7.5% of Fortune 500 top earners;

- 14.1% of Fortune 500 executive officers; and

- 16.1% of Fortune 500 board directors.

In addition, less than one-fifth of Fortune 500 companies have 25% or more women directors and about one-tenth have no women serving on their boards.

And then here is something else sobering to consider. Robin Ely, the Warren Alpert Professor of Business at Harvard Business School—and co-author of a 2011 article that proposes a fresh approach to training women leaders—has said, "Women's progress has really leveled off, and has been stuck for at least 10 years."

Unfortunately, the outlook for future generations of women is not looking all that much better.

According to a January 2012 survey of 1,001 girls ages 8 to 17 on how they view the concept of leadership—commissioned by the Girl Scouts of the USA and conducted by GfK Roper—young women still see significant barriers to their opportunities to assume leadership positions in a country where government and businesses are still dominated by men.

Among the key findings are that three in nine girls think that while women can succeed in business, they rarely become corporate executives; and many believe they are more burdened by family than men as they try to succeed in their careers.

Second-generation gender bias

I am not a social scientist and I don't pretend to know all the reasons why a stubborn glass ceiling still exists for women business leaders—but I know that it does.

Professor Ely of Harvard and her colleagues cite what they call second-generation forms of subtle gender bias as one of the reasons for the lack of women's progress. Some examples of this are stereotypical beliefs about women—for example, that women have friendly, emotional, unselfish traits—that are inconsistent with conventional wisdom of what a leader should be.

Other examples are the judgments many organizations make about who is committed to the company and who is not, which often fail to take into account the reality of women's lives. A woman with children, for example, may be less free to work nights and weekends, travel frequently or accept a new position in a different city than a man with children.

Personally I believe that both women and men would benefit if companies recognized that having a rich personal or family life does not mean an individual is less committed to her or his job. I also agree that companies must do more than simply acknowledge this statement to be true; they must change the business practices that have created systematic career obstacles for women.

On this point, I commend the Board of Directors of Yahoo!, the struggling Internet leader, for naming Marissa Mayer as its new CEO in July 2012. Mayer, an enormously talented former Google Vice President, was pregnant with her first child, due in October—a fact the Board knew when they made the appointment and that did not dissuade them from their decision.

Now you might wonder why I am stressing the obligation of organizations to make changes that make them more open to women leaders. What about women themselves? Aren't they responsible for their own careers and figuring out ways to advance? Of course they are.

And as role models, there are numerous examples of women who have risen to the very top of their professions entirely on their own against great odds or with the help of strong mentors, both male and female.

In my own career, I have had the great privilege of working with some of these women. Most notable are Anne Mulcahy, former Chairman and CEO of Xerox and her protégée, Ursula Burns, who succeeded Anne as Chairman and CEO of Xerox; Shelly Lazarus who, after 40 years with the advertising giant Ogilvy & Mather, just retired as Chairman this year (Shelly was the successor to the firm's first female CEO, Charlotte Beers); and Anita Roddick, founder of The Body Shop and a human rights advocate who pioneered corporate social responsibility and activism.

"The Accidental CEO"

I wrote about Anne Mulcahy in my first book as an example of a great leader. At the time, Anne was Chairman and CEO of Xerox Corporation, an iconic company that invented the photocopier and had such a strong brand that even today people in offices use the word "xerox" as a synonym for photocopy.

But in 1999, in the face of relentless competition, Xerox had lost its way. The company had failed to make the important transition from analog to digital copying and had wandered into ventures far removed from its core competencies.

I met Anne when I started consulting with Xerox on ways to revitalize the Xerox brand and bring back the spirit—and the fact—of innovation that made Xerox a leader in the first place. There was hardly a day in all the time I worked with Xerox that I didn't enjoy it. Xerox is an amazing company with a remarkable story and a nearly unparalleled list of accomplishments.

But back then, recognizing that a change in leadership was needed, Xerox Chairman and CEO Paul Allaire stepped down as CEO and tapped a relative outsider who had joined the company just two years prior to take his place. In May 2000, less than 13 months later and with Xerox worse off than ever, Allaire was forced to step back in as CEO. As his No. 2 person, Allaire selected Anne, naming her President of Xerox—sending a clear signal that she would be his successor as CEO.

Everyone was surprised by Allaire's pick—no one more so than Anne herself. A 24-year veteran of Xerox, Anne had spent most of her career in sales. She held English and Journalism degrees from Marymount College. She had never aspired to the job of CEO and little in her professional or educational background suggested that she would be right for it. But in 2001, she became CEO and in 2002, she was named Chairman.

So unlikely was Anne's rise to the top spot at Xerox that *Fortune* magazine called her "The Accidental CEO."

When I wrote about Anne in 2005, she was well known for having executed an aggressive turn-around plan that returned the company to profitability, decreased debt, increased cash and emphasized investment in R&D. She had weathered an SEC scandal not of her making, cleaning house financially in the process. And she was well on her way to reshaping the company, which had been on the verge of disaster.

What was less known then—at least outside of Xerox— was that Anne had early on tapped a key Xerox executive to work with her on the turnaround, a woman named Ursula Burns.

Ursula first worked at Xerox as a summer intern in 1980 and joined the company full time a year later after obtaining a Master of Science degree in mechanical engineering from Columbia University. When Anne became President of Xerox in 2000, Ursula was Vice President of Global Manufacturing. Anne promoted her to Senior Vice President and, by their own admission, the two women formed a true partnership around the task of restructuring Xerox.

Anne spent her days (and nights) externally focused— working with bankers to clean up the balance sheet, strengthening ties with customers and divesting unwanted businesses. Meanwhile Ursula tackled internal problems such as how to cut costs to free up cash to invest in R&D—without killing the company.

CEO in her own right

In 2007, as part of a well-planned succession, Ursula was named President of Xerox. In 2009, Anne retired as CEO and Ursula was named CEO—becoming the first African-American woman to head a Fortune 500 company and the first woman to succeed another woman as the head of a Fortune 500 company. In May 2010, Ursula was named Chairman of Xerox.

While the Xerox Anne turned over to Ursula when she became CEO in 2009 was in a much stronger position financially, there was still much work to be done. Neither woman was satisfied with the company's growth rate and had been seeking ways to jumpstart revenue.

The night before Ursula's first day as CEO, she and Anne got the news that Affiliated Computer Services (ACS), a $6 billion company in business process outsourcing (BPO) and IT services, had agreed to be acquired by Xerox.

Xerox had already acquired two small BPO firms in 2007, but Anne and Ursula had realized that rolling up a handful of small acquisitions was not going to be sufficient to handle the large complex business processes customers needed. The acquisition of ACS doubled

Xerox's size and increased what the company earned from services to nearly half its annual revenue. Despite some skepticism from Wall Street, the combination is showing results.

While the final chapter on the Xerox turnaround has yet to be written, at the center of it are two women leaders making history. As Ursula has said, "Some companies talk about transformation; we're actually doing it."

The other transformation led by Anne and Ursula was one that helped change forever the notion that women might not be capable of running Fortune 500 companies.

"Do you know me?"

Ogilvy & Mather has handled American Express' advertising since 1962. The firm was founded by the late David Ogilvy—arguably the most famous and clear-thinking genius in the history of advertising—in 1948.

Shelly Lazarus, who retired in 2012 after 40 years with Ogilvy & Mather, doesn't go back that far. She joined Ogilvy & Mather when David was active in the firm, and was mentored and counseled by him until his death in 1998.

But here is the point of my story. For many years she was an indispensable and consistent contributor in one after another of American Express' extraordinary advertising campaigns. Without her, they wouldn't have been so extraordinary.

Many American Express ad campaigns, slogans and TV commercials that haven't appeared in 20, 30 or even 40 years are remembered as if they were seen just last week. We all remember the impact of:

- "Do You Know Me?"
- "Membership Has Its Privileges"
- "Portraits," with photographs by Annie Leibowitz
- "Don't Leave Home Without It"

These campaigns are recognized among the top 100 advertising campaigns of the 20th century.

American Express could not have done all of this without Shelly. She and others at Ogilvy & Mather worked with us to create a superb partnership based on a professional relationship supported by personal relationships characterized by mutual trust, affection, respect and common purpose.

So it was no surprise to me when Shelly was named CEO of Ogilvy & Mather Worldwide in 1996, and added the title of Chairman in 1997, after nearly 30 years with the firm.

In retrospect, perhaps Shelly's rise to CEO should have been a surprise. Even in the 1990s, most CEOs of top ad agencies were men. But Shelly was not the first female CEO of Ogilvy & Mather. She succeeded Charlotte Beers, a larger-than-life personality who is rightly credited with paving the way for women in the hyper-competitive world of advertising.

Charlotte was the first woman vice president of J. Walter Thompson in the firm's 106-year history. She later served as CEO of ad agency Tatham-Laird & Kudner before joining Ogilvy & Mather in 1992 as CEO. In 1997, Charlotte was the first woman to appear on the cover of *Fortune* magazine, in its first issue featuring the most powerful women in America. From 2001-2003, she served as Undersecretary of State for Public Diplomacy & Public Affairs.

I had the pleasure of working with Charlotte from time to time while she was at Ogilvy & Mather. But it was Shelly with whom I spent many years in the trenches on some of the most challenging and gratifying work of my career. So indelibly intertwined was she with American Express that she once told me that for many years her children thought she worked there.

Charlotte and Shelly could not have been more different in their working styles. Both were effective. But as outgoing and flamboyant as Charlotte was, Shelly was all about quiet competence.

In many ad agencies, leaders often are heroes of the save-the-day variety. But when Shelly was around, heroics weren't necessary. The day did not have to be saved. When you worked with Shelly, what you got was a smart, civilized, supremely professional, top-quality experience that made everyone feel good about being part of the team.

Shelly's leadership style was strongly influenced by David Ogilvy, whose greatest advice to her was so compatible with her own personal values that it fit like a hand in a glove. In her own words:

"Like many great companies, O&M has a very value-driven culture. When I hear people talk disparagingly, even if humorously, about people they work with or about their clients, I know that person won't do well here. We have such inherent respect for each other and for our clients. It might work elsewhere—in fact, there are agencies that pride themselves on that attitude—but it just doesn't work here."

"Constructive lunacy"

Long before *Fortune* magazine began publishing an annual ranking of the world's largest companies according to how well they conform to socially responsible business practices, there was Anita Roddick and The Body Shop.

I had the pleasure—and the challenge—of working with Anita for five years as a member of the Board of Directors of The Body Shop. One of the world's most successful retailers of cosmetics, The Body Shop sought my advice on the company's branding and advertising strategy.

I use the word "pleasure" because Anita was one of the most brilliant entrepreneurs and marketers I have ever worked with. I say "challenge" because she was so energetic and passionate and fiercely committed to doing things a different way—her way—that she could be difficult to work with.

Anita called her mode of working "constructive lunacy," which she explained this way: "The difference between the crazy person and the successful entrepreneur is, of course, that the latter can convince others to share the vision. That force of will is fundamental to entrepreneurship. Like a genie in a bottle, the idea is nothing unless someone can exploit it, which is another thing that separates entrepreneurs from everyone else."

When Anita passed away in 2007 from a brain hemorrhage, the world lost a trailblazer and a role model whose efforts paved the way for generations of social entrepreneurs and activists who have created businesses that "do well by doing good."

The story of how The Body Shop came to be is well known. In the mid-1970s, Anita and her husband Gordon Roddick were the parents of two young daughters, eking out a hard living running a restaurant and a small hotel in southern England. Overwhelmed and overworked, Gordon told Anita that he needed a break and, with her approval, set out on a 10-month trek on horseback from Buenos Aires to New York. Anita was left to support herself and her children.

Scrambling for a way to earn a living, Anita began experimenting with how to create cosmetics using everyday ingredients found in her home. With her kitchen serving as her laboratory, Anita developed her first dozen or so products. Using her hotel as collateral, she opened a shop in Brighton to sell them. By the time Gordon had returned from his trek, she had opened a second shop. The rest, as they say, is history.

(By the way, Anita's kitchen continued to play a central role in the growth and success of The Body Shop. I recall many meetings of The Body Shop's Board of Directors that were held in the kitchen of her London home.)

Today, The Body Shop has more than 2,000 stores in 50 different markets around the world. In 2006, the company was acquired by the L'Oréal Group, but remained independently managed.

Anita founded The Body Shop to provide a living for herself and her children. But it also provided an opportunity for Anita to express her strongly held beliefs about social justice and corporate responsibility.

International travel before her marriage had exposed her to women's body rituals in many countries, many of which involved using natural and locally available ingredients. Further—having observed her mother's frugality during World War II—she would reuse containers whenever possible rather than throwing them away. In fact from the beginning Anita questioned many existing retail business practices about merchandising and packaging.

The Body Shop's environmental activism was born out of what she learned from these experiences.

Anita also was a trailblazer in the fair trade movement in the cosmetics world, establishing direct relationships with communities in developing countries that would become suppliers to The Body Shop. The company was the first international cosmetics brand to be recognized under the Humane Cosmetics Standard for its policy against animal testing.

In addition to the company's core values, supported by its business practices, Anita was active personally in causes of her own. When she stepped down as Co-Chairman of The Body Shop in 2002, she spent 80 days of the year working as a consultant in her stores and used the rest of her time to campaign against human rights abuses and exploitation of the underprivileged.

Anita's groundbreaking philosophy of the purpose in business is best expressed in her own words:

"I believe that there's a better way. It is possible to trade ethically, to commit to global social responsibility. I still think it's possible to rewrite the rulebook. That was always the vision. It's about creating a new business paradigm and showing that business can have a human face. It's about empowering employees—without being scared of them—as the key to keeping them, and empowering them by creating a more inclusive system. It's about demonstrating that you will not forsake your values at the cost of your workforce. It's about paying attention to the aesthetics of business. It's all that. You may not get there, but at least you try to make the journey an honorable one."

When historians write about the birth of social activism in business, two companies are often portrayed as pioneers. One is Ben & Jerry's, the American ice cream company founded in 1978 whose founders adopted socially responsible business practices from the start and used some of the profits their company generated to promote social causes. Founded in 1976, The Body Shop is often the other example.

Through The Body Shop and her own personal causes, Anita will long be remembered as someone who literally redefined business as we know it.

What about all the other capable women?

I write in such detail about my experiences with each of these exceptional women because they taught me two things. First, each of them succeeded through sheer strength of will and character and against all odds. Second, they prove that women business leaders are as talented and varied in their skills, approaches and leadership styles as their male counterparts.

The stories of these women leaders also remind me that as stellar as their careers and accomplishments have been, there are many more women who are fully capable of rising through the ranks and achieving leadership roles. But they are stymied by systemic and societal barriers that force them to make tradeoffs. Many ultimately take another path.

This must change—not just so women can achieve the career success they would like, but also so business can benefit from the talent and skills of more than half the population.

Now when I look at the miniscule number of women who have achieved leadership positions in American business, I know that clearly what we've been doing is not working. And what we've been doing, by and large, is encouraging women who wish to reach the top simply to emulate their male colleagues and hope for the best.

The problem with that advice is that today's male business leaders are judged by performance standards set by men whose own performance was judged by standards set by men and so on, reaching back for generations.

In a book about the power of reinvention, I would be remiss in not taking businesses to task on the question of women leaders. At a time when companies are seeking new ways to grow and enter new markets—and serve existing markets better—the need for creative thinking and deep understanding of customers and employees has never been greater. In the face of this need, there is no better time to bring more women into our companies in leadership positions.

And so I must ask: isn't it time we created environments in which capable women can succeed?

What can businesses gain by hiring veterans returning from Iraq and Afghanistan?

Can we tap into new military leadership and work styles—developed during two wars unlike any others we have experienced—to solve the business challenges we face today?

Roughly 2.4 million American men and women have served in the Iraq and Afghanistan wars—the longest military operations since the Vietnam War. About 1.4 million now have separated from the military and are back in civilian life.

Unlike GIs returning from World War II—who came home to an exciting period of economic transformation, jobs, subsidized education and home ownership programs—the picture for veterans of these Middle East conflicts is mixed.

Here is one example. According to the U.S. Bureau of Labor Statistics, in June 2012 the unemployment rate for Iraq and Afghanistan veterans was 9.5%. This compared to a national unemployment rate of 8.2%.

Throughout the economic downturn, unemployment rates for the men and women returning from service in these conflicts have been consistently higher than the national average. For veterans 24 years old and younger, the rate has sometimes been more than three times higher.

Why are returning veterans having such a hard time finding jobs?

One reason is that some potential employers are wary of hiring people who have gone through the shock of combat and the stress of multiple tours of duty. A 2010 poll by the Society for Human Resource Management of 429 human resources managers and recruiters found that 41% were concerned about veterans' mental health (one in four vets of these wars suffers from depression or post-traumatic stress disorder). An even larger concern than health—expressed by 60%—was that transferring military skills to the civilian workplace could be a challenge.

While these fears are understandable, I believe they point to a need for people to know more about returning veterans. For despite the views of some, many hiring managers believe ex-military personnel make excellent employees and are good for their businesses.

This was the conclusion drawn from detailed and lengthy interviews with 87 individuals representing 69 companies conducted in 2010 by the Center for New American Security.

Participants were large companies with operations throughout the United States and globally, and from many different industries. The list included companies such as AT&T, Boeing, Cisco, Facebook, Kraft Foods, Procter & Gamble, Target and Waste Management. Of the companies interviewed, 51% have formal programs for hiring vets while 62% formally target veterans for hire.

Traits of returning veterans appealing to these major employers, reported in the study, include:

- Leadership and teamwork skills

- Positive character traits such as trustworthiness, dependability and a strong work ethic

- Structure and discipline

- Expertise, and job-related occupational skills and experience

- The ability to perform and make decisions in rapidly changing circumstances

- Relative comfort working in difficult environments, and with travel and relocating for work

- Loyalty to the organizations for which they work

These positive qualities were attributed to veterans generally. Those who have experienced combat are singled out for additional recognition. One consistent observation: they don't rattle easily.

A typical comment along these lines: a business crisis just doesn't seem stressful in comparison.

But here is something else that is interesting. Where the military really seems to excel is in its ability to train leaders.

This might come as a surprise to anyone whose image of military leadership is a stone-faced man in a crisply starched uniform barking orders at hapless teenaged troops whose job—it is absolutely clear—begins and ends with doing what they're told. In other words, some people believe that military leadership is long on command and control and short on interpersonal skills.

But in the modern military—while the chain of command is still very important—up-and-coming leaders are more often trained to think for themselves and to think on their feet. They are drilled not to take orders blindly but instead to understand that while the mission must be made clear to the individuals under their command, changing conditions require giving them the freedom to be resourceful and creative when it comes to how that mission can be achieved.

They are taught that the difference between defeat and victory is often one decision at a pivotal moment in time.

Michael Useem, Professor of Management and Director of the Center for Leadership and Change

Management at the Wharton School, University of Pennsylvania, routinely incorporates military leadership principles into his MBA and executive MBA programs. He calls this idea of key decisions at critical junctures "The Leadership Moment." In his book of the same name, he presents nine stories of leaders who faced such a moment—and either performed brilliantly or spectacularly failed.

One of the stories Professor Useem tells in the book is from the Civil War. It's about Joshua Lawrence Chamberlain, a 34-year-old officer in the Union army who fought in the Battle of Gettysburg.

A Professor of Modern Languages at Bowdoin College in Maine, Chamberlain had no military education or training. But he believed so strongly in the Union's cause that in the summer of 1862 he took a leave of absence from teaching and enlisted. At first offered the rank of colonel and command of the 20th Maine Regiment, he declined, saying he preferred to start at a lower rank so he "could learn." So instead, he was named a lieutenant colonel of the regiment.

Less than a year later, having distinguished himself in several battles, he was promoted to colonel of the regiment when the existing man retired.

At Gettysburg, on the second day of the battle, the Confederates sensed the vulnerability of the Union forces and mounted a new attack against its left flank. Chamberlain's commander placed him and his 400 soldiers on the southern slope of a hill called Little Round Top at the end point of the Union line—making it clear that if the Confederate attackers managed to get through the line, all would be lost.

Chamberlain was told in no uncertain terms to hold the line, no matter what. But while the commander was very clear about what Chamberlain's mission was, he did not say how it should be achieved.

The Confederates began their attack. After two hours of holding the line, Chamberlain's troops had sustained numerous casualties and were nearly out of ammunition. Chamberlain had minutes to make a decision about what to do next. He ordered his left wing to fix their bayonets on their empty muskets and charge down the hill, swinging back and forth as if on a hinge—a movement that created a simultaneous frontal assault and a flanking maneuver.

The Confederates were stunned by this completely unexpected action. Chamberlain and his troops saved the flank, capturing more than 100 Confederate soldiers in the process.

For his bravery and inventiveness, Chamberlain was awarded the Medal of Honor, the military's highest recognition.

Military leadership training—a 200-year tradition

How is it that the U.S. military can produce leaders of the caliber of Joshua Lawrence Chamberlain?

For starters, the concept of leadership training is relatively new in business—historians trace its origins to the 1930s—but the U.S. military has been at it for more than 200 years. President Thomas Jefferson signed legislation establishing the U.S. Military Academy at West Point in 1802.

With more than 65,000 alumni, West Point has produced two Presidents of the United States (Ulysses S. Grant and Dwight D. Eisenhower); the President of the Confederate States of America, Jefferson Davis; and many notable generals from William Tecumsah Sherman (Civil War) to John J. Pershing (World War I) to George S. Patton (World War II) to David Petraeus (Middle East conflicts and currently Director of the Central Intelligence Agency).

The seeds of military leadership training took root in the late 1700s, sparked by the American Revolutionary

War and advances in military technology that gave field forces more mobility. With mobility came more options for how battles could be fought. And that gave rise to a doctrine called "mission orders"—an excellent example being the instructions given to Chamberlain by his commanding officer at Gettysburg.

American military manuals define a mission order as "an order to a unit to perform a mission without specifying how it will be accomplished." Similarly, Marine doctrine is expressed this way: "We leave the manner of accomplishing the mission to the subordinate, thereby allowing him the freedom and establishing the duty for him to take whatever steps deemed necessary based on the situation. The senior prescribes the method of execution only to the degree that is essential for coordination."

In business, we call this "delegating"—an idea that can be simply stated yet is extraordinarily challenging to implement.

Delegating has the advantage of allowing organizations to be more responsive to changing situations. It also speeds execution because decisions are made at the point of action. The disadvantage is that lower level leaders must be trained to read situations and act appropriately instead of just following orders.

At the same time senior leaders must abandon the notion of themselves as the ones most capable of doing the job and instead put their confidence in the younger people who report to them. They also must learn the nuanced art of making "the mission" clear—without dictating the details—through superb and often inspiring communication.

Military service and business leadership

With such a strong tradition of leadership training in the military, it is no surprise that many Americans who have served in the military go on to distinguished careers as leaders in civilian life. After the Civil War ended, Joshua Lawrence Chamberlain was elected to four one-year terms as the Governor of Maine and later returned to Bowdoin College, where he would become its president.

More recently, a 2006 report from Korn/Ferry, the world's largest executive search firm, and the Economist Intelligence Unit found that 8.4% of CEOs of the Standard & Poor's 500 had been in the military. This compared with just 3% of American males who had served in the armed forces.

Why the over-representation? From the report: "There are clearly certain traits ex-military CEOs possess that drive their approaches to leadership, communication and, perhaps most importantly, the ability to translate company vision into tangible results."

It is only fair to note that the number of CEOs with military backgrounds actually has declined dramatically over the last two decades as World War II and Korean War veterans have begun to retire. In 1980, 59% of the CEOs of large publicly held corporations had served in the military.

This, of course, is a reflection of short supply caused by the move from conscripted to voluntary service rather than a sudden decline in the quality of military leaders. About 13 million Americans served during World War II compared with 2.7 million in Vietnam and, as previously mentioned, 2.4 million in Iraq and Afghanistan.

It is interesting that most of the CEOs interviewed in the Korn/Ferry study preferred a military background to an MBA. GE CEO Jeff Immelt, who did not serve in the military—at 56 years old he would have been too young to serve in Vietnam—nevertheless has said he admires the qualities and skills of former military personnel, and especially their ability to "deal with ambiguity."

Ex-military CEOs themselves are even more certain that the leadership skills they learned in the military were essential to their success. Fred Smith, Founder, Chairman and CEO of FedEx, and a Marine in Vietnam from 1967 to 1970, has said: "I do not believe I could have built FedEx without the skills I learned from the Marine Corps. The Corps altered my life, and I have always been grateful to it."

Bob Stevens, Chairman and CEO of Lockheed Martin, also a former Marine who served in Vietnam, has said: "I did not learn about leadership in business school. I learned about leadership when I was 18 years old and first introduced to the United States Marine Corps where leadership is not taught by a favored professor in a three-credit hour course. It is taught by every officer and every NCO (non-commissioned officer) in every minute and every hour of every day, in every action, every word, every deed, and every circumstance."

The list of veterans of that generation who became CEOs is long. It includes A.G. Lafley, retired Chairman and CEO of Procter & Gamble; Daniel Akerson, Chairman and CEO of General Motors; and Donald Graham, Chairman and CEO of the Washington Post Company.

More to the story

But the nature of conflicts has changed since World War II, the Korean War and Vietnam, and so has business. Therefore it's right to ask: does the current generation of returning veterans have the leadership skills it will take to help American businesses solve today's challenges?

In my view, the answer is, "Absolutely."

I write and speak extensively about different leadership styles. And I often contrast the heroic definition of leadership that many of us grew up with—Alexander the Great, larger than life in gleaming armor on a tall white horse, dominating the battlefield with his fearless presence—with our need today for an empowered workforce able to take initiative and responsibility.

In my first book, to illustrate the latter style, I wrote about Chris Hughes, a young lieutenant colonel in Iraq. Hughes was featured in an article by Dan Baum in the January 17, 2005 issue of the *New Yorker* called "Battle Lessons: What the Generals Don't Know."

You may recall that when faced with his own leadership moment—a mob of Iraqis in the city of Najaf furious because they believed the soldiers were about to attack their mosque—Hughes stepped between the Iraqis and his men with his weapon pointed toward the ground. He then ordered his men to point their own weapons to the ground, drop to one knee and…smile and relax.

Both sides were surprised by the action, even his men. But they obeyed. The action demonstrated to the Iraqis that the soldiers meant no harm to either them or their mosque. Witnesses to the event are convinced that a confrontation that could have ended in a bloody massacre was completely defused by Hughes' quick thinking and calm demeanor.

But there is more to the story—and more to say about the type of military leadership that evolved, out of necessity, during the conflict in Iraq. Consider this:

- Soldiers trained as an attack force had to function as an occupation force.

- Trained to fight in large-scale open warfare, they were instead fighting in small units in city streets.

- Trained to fight, they spent much of their time on civilian projects—fixing sewer systems and running town councils.

They didn't speak the language. They couldn't tell the enemy from innocent civilians. Everything changed constantly. There was never a moment when they were free of danger.

In conditions such as those in Iraq, no previous body of knowledge or experience existed that could spell out what might work and what might not. In the absence of prescribed procedures, young officers had to improvise on their own.

The bottom line is that most of them did their jobs extremely well, showing amazing ingenuity and initiative.

Expanding on the story of Chris Hughes, he was no stranger to Muslim customs having been part of the team investigating the bombing of the U.S.S. Cole in Yemen and serving on an anti-terrorism task force. But when he found out that he and his soldiers were heading for Najaf, he took the initiative to learn more about the people who lived there and the grand Ali Mosque in the city, which was considered a most holy site.

Over the course of a 54-hour journey by truck to the city, he peppered his Iraqi-English translator with questions. By the time he arrived, he understood how important the mosque was to the residents of Najaf.

This no doubt influenced the decision he made at that crucial moment when an angry mob confronted his unit.

A few months after the incident, the *New Yorker* writer tracked down Hughes in his native Iowa and asked him to explain his thinking on that day.

Hughes said he figured the Iraqis might calm down if the Americans made a gesture showing they respected the mosque and wouldn't attack it. There were no such gestures available to him in a military operating manual. So he improvised the order to his men: get out of fighting stance…turn your weapon upside-down…drop to one knee.

Just think about that scene for a moment. The anger of the mob…the edginess of his men…all eyes on him. Most of us will go through our whole career without coming up with such a brilliant solution under maximum pressure.

Adaptive military leadership gains legitimacy

In a superb article that appeared in *Time* magazine in August 2011, investigative writer Joe Klein wrote that the two Middle East wars required a new military skill set, far more sophisticated than for previous wars, and far more than the "yes-sir, no-sir rote discipline that most civilians associated with the military."

Klein quoted John Nagl, a retired lieutenant colonel in the U.S. Army and now a research fellow at the U.S. Naval Academy: "World War I was fought by large units like battalions. World War II was fought by companies… Vietnam, by platoons. The current wars are all about small teams who have to interact with the local Iraqi and Afghan populations. That has required a different kind of soldier."

It has also required a different kind of leadership—and a different kind of leadership training. That too has evolved during the course of these two Middle East wars, and has been refined into a new model for a leadership style some call "adaptive leadership."

What is interesting about adaptive leadership in today's military is that it was first demonstrated in the field by Chris Hughes and other young officers in Iraq and Afghanistan and later would be studied and introduced as a formal part of armed forces training.

That effort was led by General David Petraeus, a four-star general with 37 years of service in the U.S. Army before he retired in 2010. Petraeus' last assignments before retiring were commanding vast U.S. military forces in Iraq, CENTCOM (the U.S. central command over the Middle East) and Afghanistan.

As a major general with the 101st Airborne Division in 2003 in Iraq, Petraeus understood the distinctly different nature of the conflict from ones that U.S. forces had seen in previous wars. He studied the mistakes of other leaders who had faced insurgencies before him, and concluded that it is not possible to counter an insurgency with military force alone. He developed a new approach based on winning over the Iraqi people.

Above all, Petraeus saw that the greatest need was to protect the local civilian populations in Iraq from insurgents. So he adopted a strategy of troops being actively present among the population to provide security for the people.

Petraeus also saw a need for nation building in Iraq. He used his discretionary funds to build schools, establish work projects and support local elections. He helped reopen the University of Mosul and built local alliances to help establish military security for civilians. This brought an end to Al–Qaeda's control of local populations in those regions.

From 2005 to 2007, Petraeus was responsible for over-seeing Army schools, centers and training programs. He also was responsible for and co-authored the Army's doctrinal manuals, used to train the Army's officers, and supervised the Army's center for the collection and dis-semination of lessons learned. He took his new ideas about counterinsurgency strategies with him.

In 2006 Petraeus and his team re-wrote the book—literally, it was a field manual—on counterinsurgency, integrating much of what they had learned into lesson plans and training exercises. John Nagl worked along-side Petraeus during this time and was a member of the team that wrote the manual.

Nagl credits Petraeus' "mental construct" of how to counter an insurgency, and his recognition that sol-diers in Iraq and Afghanistan were performing duties far beyond what they had been trained for, as reasons for the military's renewed belief in the importance of teaching soldiers how to think, and of fostering flexibil-ity and adaptability in leaders.

As a result, there are a growing number of people who believe that, if anything, the leadership skills of the men and women returning from Iraq and Afghanistan are even more relevant to the challenges faced by business leaders today. As Klein wrote in *Time,* "Veterans returning from both Iraq and Afghanistan bring skills that are exactly what America needs right now: crisp decision making, rigor, optimism, entrepreneurial creativity and a larger sense of purpose."

Another proponent of that point of view is Tom Kolditz, a retired brigadier general and PhD in Social Psychology. For 12 years, Kolditz led the Department of Behavioral Sciences and Leadership at West Point. He now is a senior lecturer at Yale University's School of Management. One of his favorite topics is the military's success in developing a new generation of real-world leaders with skills that should be as welcome in the boardroom as they were on the battlefield.

Writing in the *Harvard Business Review* in 2009, Colonel Kolditz noted four ways in which today's military prepares leaders that business would benefit from:

#1 Extensive preparation: The military spends far more time preparing for missions—evaluating many possible scenarios and how they might play out—than it does carrying the missions out.

In business, of course, the reverse is true.

#2 Training up: The military has learned that if you don't train your leaders at all levels properly—which means training them for decision making several levels above their pay grade—you can't delegate authority and expect to reap the benefits.

In business, training is often narrowly specific to the job or task at hand.

#3 Powering down: The military teaches decision making by creating a simple but flexible system of having leaders in training make lots of decisions in simulated situations and then critiquing the outcomes. The result is that a freshly minted second lieutenant is usually more adept at decision making than many mid-level managers in business.

Most decision-making training in business consists of working for long periods of time on a few large case studies—emphasizing depth over agility, analysis over informed action.

#4 Comprehensive debriefing: The military thoroughly debriefs after each mission, examining decisions and outcomes and how different decisions could have produced a different result...learning from mistakes.

In business, post mortems often are pro forma.

The bottom line is that in today's military conflicts, adaptability is vital to survival. As business leaders must cope with fast change and increasing unpredictability, one could easily say the same for them.

Now to be clear, I'm not in favor of throwing away careful strategies in favor of improvising. Improvising is a valuable talent but not a strategy—it's something you do when strategy is interrupted by reality.

And obviously it would be ridiculous to compare the environments of Iraq and Afghanistan to anything business leaders face doing business in the United States. I am not trying to force a false metaphor between war and business.

What I am suggesting is that returning veterans merit serious consideration by American businesses looking for our next generation of leaders. That's because to a large extent the young men and women who are today's military officers do exactly what most business leaders do.

They provide frontline, small-unit leadership in relentlessly challenging situations.

What do Millennials need and want to be successful?

How must leadership and working styles change as our next-generation leaders enter the workforce and assume positions of responsibility?

Four days before Facebook went public on May 18, 2012—opening with a staggering $104 billion valuation—Founder and CEO Mark Zuckerberg celebrated his birthday. At 28 he is the youngest Fortune 500 CEO—12 years younger than the CEO who previously held that distinction, Google's Larry Page.

Much has been written about Zuckerberg during Facebook's meteoric rise. He was born in Dobbs Ferry, New York, the oldest of four children. He developed an interest in computers at an early age. By his mid-teens, he was taking graduate level courses in programming at a college near his home.

After attending a prestigious private high school, Zuckerberg went on to Harvard. Like two other fantastically successful young entrepreneurs who came before him—Bill Gates of Microsoft and Steve Jobs of Apple—he dropped out of college to work on what would become Facebook.

Zuckerberg may have intentionally stolen the idea for Facebook from classmates who created its precursor, a site called Harvard Connection. Hollywood made a movie about it. Stubborn court battles continue.

When Facebook was about to go public, Zuckerberg's participation in the time-honored tradition of making pitches to potential investors was minimal. When he did show up, he was wearing his trademark hoodie—the urban version of the traditional, zip-up-the-front cotton sweatshirt with a hood. This rankled Wall Street, making headlines for days.

The day after the Facebook IPO—when Zuckerberg's personal net-worth grew to about $17 billion—he married his girlfriend of eight years, Priscilla Chan. She recently graduated from medical school and plans to become a pediatrician.

The couple has a dog, Beast, who has his own Facebook page. Beast has attracted more than 1,000,000 "likes" since joining Facebook in March 2011.

For all the things you know about Mark Zuckerberg, here is something you might not have realized: he is the first Millennial CEO of a Fortune 500 company.

And whether you admire or disdain Zuckerberg, this is a very important milestone. Here's why.

Millennials and their rising influence

Also known as Generation Y, Millennials were born sometime between the early 1980s and the mid-to-late 1990s. Experts disagree on the exact timeframe.

More important than the precise dates bracketing this generation is its size. There are more Millennials even than Baby Boomers—80-something million compared with 70-something million—or about one-fourth of the total U.S. population. By some estimates 10,000 Millennials turn 21 years old every day in America.

There may already be as many as 40 million Millennials in the U.S. workforce. By 2014 they are expected to make up more than half of American workers. By 2025, three out of four workers globally will be Millennials.

Now as we all know, each generation makes its own mark on our culture and society. In that respect Millennials will be no different. But the sheer numbers of people born in this generation give Millennials more power than most to challenge cultural norms and remake society.

So while Mark Zuckerberg is the first Millennial CEO of a Fortune 500 company, he is just the first of many, many more to come. As a business leader, for that reason alone, you need to learn all you can about Millennials.

But here is something else to consider. Millennials are not just coming to work for your company: they are going to change the rules—about how you recruit, compensate and reward, manage, communicate, and interact—how you *do* what you do and perhaps even *what* you do.

And as someone who has worn a business suit and tie every day to work for 50 years, as much as I hate to say it, they are going to change what you wear.

Here are several reasons why.

While not all Millennials were born digital, technology is an integral part of their daily lives. When many of today's business leaders were young, media meant print, radio, and television; and technology meant computers housed in air-cooled rooms with raised floors and ceilings, programmed by bright, yet eccentric, young men.

In contrast Millennials have grown up in an extremely media- and technology-rich world. They have never watched television without a remote control. Personal computers, video games and the Internet became commonplace in their childhoods. Mobile technology—handheld games, music players and phones—has been around since they were pre-teens and, for some, even younger.

As a result Millennials are always connected: in constant communication or interacting with friends on social sites or on their mobile phones texting or talking.

And while they still consume traditional content such as music, film and television, Millennials also produce it—mixing, remixing and sharing multimedia narrations and interpretations of their lives and the world around them.

Largely because of their use of technology, Millennials are natural connectors and collaborators, comfortable with forming and being a part of teams and communities. And where community once was defined by geography or perhaps political or religious beliefs, Millennials experience community around a wide range of ideas and interests—and across continents and cultures.

Millennials are ethnically and racially diverse. According to U.S. Census data, one in three is a member of a group considered a minority—Hispanic, African-American or Asian. Nine of ten have friends outside their ethnic group.

Reflecting themselves and the world that surrounds them, many Millennials simply don't understand older generations' perspectives on race, religion and hot-button social issues. Ethnic, cultural and social diversity is just part of their lives and they are tolerant of all types of diversity around them.

Numerous studies show that Millennials are motivated to make a difference in the world. They do this by recycling, volunteering, educating friends and family about the environment, donating money to social causes and by starting their own socially responsible companies.

Millennials extend these commitments to the companies they purchase goods and services from. They are more conscientious consumers than previous generations, demanding greater accountability and transparency from businesses and more positive participation in the communities in which they do business. In these actions Millennials are reshaping corporate America's ethics and conduct.

Millennials are not content to follow the status quo. Instead they have their sights set on visiting places never before visited, discovering new truths and proving there is another—better—way. They prize inventiveness, creativity and independence. They are the most entrepreneurial generation yet.

While much of this sounds appealing, Millennials can also be challenging, both as customers and employees. Some of the attributes described above are what make them challenging. So before I make my case for why you should embrace Millennials for the good of your company, let's look at how they can be frustrating.

What's wrong with Millennials?

Every generation has its complaints about the younger generation. Parents complain about how their children wear their hair; the clothing styles they prefer; their taste in music; their attitudes about sex, drugs, marriage, children. No matter what age we are, we've all been there, done that—or had it done to us.

When each younger generation enters the workforce, their managers and older coworkers pick up where their parents left off.

Now it's not exactly a secret that Millennials don't have the best reputation in the workplace. Among the most popular criticisms:

◉ Millennials take things for granted.

Jobs are scarce for young people right now, but Millennials seem to feel they have limitless opportunities. They act like we should feel lucky to have them working for us and not for someone else!

◉ Millennials never just do what they're told.

Millennials want to know why they are being asked to do something, how it fits into the big picture and whether there might be a better way to do it. And they are not shy about letting everyone know how they feel.

● Millennials think they're exempt from the rules.

Set work hours, coming into the office every day, dress codes, no dogs at work? Those types of workplace rules are for their parents. Millennials want flex hours, they want to work at home or at Starbucks sometimes, every day should be casual Friday, and Scout at the office would be "no trouble at all."

● Millennials are arrogant.

Give a Millennial a new job with more responsibility, and instead of being grateful, they act as if they should have had the job all along. And what's wrong with you for taking so long to recognize their talent, skills and great ideas?

● Millennials don't want to pay their dues.

Millennials want all the good things in life, but they don't want to earn them. There no such phrase as "entry-level" in their vocabularies. Why should anything they do ever be dull, routine or boring? Hierarchies mean little. Why shouldn't everyone create graphics

for their own presentations or make their own copies…
and while we're at it, "Why can't I go to that meeting?"

● Millennials are all about instant gratification.

With Millennials, everything has to happen right
now. If one of them sends you an email and you don't
respond within 10 minutes, they'll be in your office
asking when they can expect an answer.

The other side of the story

No doubt some of these things are true of some
Millennials. Frankly they are true of some people I
encountered in my career long before Millennials were
even born! Generalizations are tricky, especially when
applied broadly to entire categories of individuals.

So, as our desire is to move beyond outrage to insight—
and perhaps even to a little appreciation—let's also look
at work from Millennials' point of view, starting with
a January 2012 study by MTV. Among the study's analysis and key findings:

◉ What some might conclude is Millennials' "career pickiness" could be an expression of a need to connect deeply with their work.

    ▸ "Loving what I do" outranked salary and a big bonus as things Millennials look for at work.

    ▸ 89% agreed that "it's important to be constantly learning at my job."

    ▸ Half of Millennials say they would rather have no job than a job they hate.

    ▸ 95% said they are motivated to work harder when they "know where their work is going."

◉ What could be misinterpreted as "self importance" is instead a deep sense of having new ideas and wanting to contribute, and a belief that learning is a two-way street.

    ▸ Millennials have been raised by "peer-ents" who encouraged them to constantly learn, grow and self actualize—a quest that extends to the workplace.

    ▸ 76% believe "my boss could learn something from me."

    ▸ 65% say they "should be mentoring older coworkers when it comes to tech and getting things done."

● While older generations prefer a separation between life and work, the ideal workplace for Millennials blends life and work "like a smoothie."

- ▸ 9 out of 10 Millennials want their workplace to be social and fun.

- ▸ 93% say they want a job where they can be themselves.

- ▸ 70% of them say they need "me" time at work (compared to 39% of Baby Boomers).

- ▸ 71% want their coworkers to be like a second family.

- ▸ Asked to draw pictures of their personal dress code at work and at play, the images were almost exactly the same.

● Instead of a career being defined as a series of jobs one performs well to earn the next, Millennials define a career as inventing great new jobs and doing them.

- ▸ 66% of Millennials want to create their own positions and responsibilities at work.

- ▸ 83% say they want a job where their creativity is valued.

❍ While older generations think of business leaders as authority figures, Millennials think of them as mentors, life coaches and guides.

  ▸ 75% of Millennials want a mentor.

Clearly, Millennials have new ideas about work, their role in the workplace and the task of leaders. They want to make a difference by helping solve important problems for their employers and perhaps even the world. Meaning is more important than money. They don't understand why you don't ask their opinions or consult them. And they want their work to be interesting and fun.

Why your company should embrace Millennials

At first some of you might resist the influence of Millennials in your company. But sooner or later you will give in—just like every generation that has come before has bowed to every generation that has followed. For no matter how hard you might try, you cannot remake Millennials in your image. Instead over time, they will reinvent your company in theirs.

In my view, this can be a good thing. Because Millennials—with their demographics, attitudes, values, unique skills and view of the world—can be superb additions to your workforce—as long as they have plenty of structure and coaching from you.

Here are a few areas where Millennials can help your company win—and some thoughts about what you can do to help them help you.

Millennials can help make your company more technology savvy. It should come as no surprise that Millennials want to work the way they live—surrounded by the exciting personal and mobile technology that gives them instantaneous access to content, information and their peers.

As a result, when they enter the workforce they may bring with them sky-high expectations about the technologies you will make available to them to do their jobs. And they will no doubt be disappointed by the reliable, but often unadventurous, technology they are likely to find in many companies today.

But of course, it isn't just about what Millennials want. Your customers too have become accustomed to instant access to information and high levels of interaction through technology in their daily lives. This is causing a fundamental shift in how they want to interact with businesses and creating completely different expectations about how—and how fast—companies will engage with them before, during and after a purchase or other type of interaction.

During these "moments of truth"—which may begin and end in minutes—a customer can be won or lost for life.

I write at length about how digital technology has changed the consumer journey in the final chapter of this book. But here is my point: meeting the technology needs of consumers in the marketplace and Millennials in the workplace is rapidly becoming one and the same. That's because on the other end of these increasingly technology-enabled interactions with customers are likely to be your new Millennial employees. It is in your company's best interests to provide them with the tools they need to make the best decisions possible in those moments of truth.

Making this shift will require companies to fundamentally rethink their technology strategies and investments. Instead of continuing to focus primarily on efficiency improvements to little-seen infrastructures, they must shift to empowering everyday business users to create insights, collaborate and take action in real time.

This is a revolutionary idea for most companies, which have tended to focus their technology initiatives on front-line workers at the edge of the enterprise or executives at the top.

Here is where Millennials can help you. They are excited to share their knowledge and expertise about technology. They are willing to give you insight and firsthand reactions to new technology trends as they emerge. They want to help coworkers who are less comfortable with technology come up to speed. And they are eager to learn new things—for example, how their technology skills can be applied to your business, your strategy and serving your customers.

Millennials can help elevate collaboration to a core competency. One of the positive outgrowths of Millennials' affinity for technology is their commitment to communicating, connecting and sharing. Their collaborative nature is evident in a wide range of activities— from researching a term paper to choosing a restaurant to deciding what music to listen to. In their daily lives, Millennials rely on social technologies and networks to learn others' opinions in the form of reviews, ratings and rankings. Sharing information freely and extending a hand to others every chance they get are just part of their everyday lives.

The good news is that Millennials bring these attitudes and skills with them to your workplace. Unlike any previous generation, Millennials arrive at your company with a built-in appreciation for the value of a peer network in making decisions and getting things done, and of the importance of contributing to the group's collective knowledge.

What do they expect in return? Usually nothing more than recognition for their contributions to the greater good—for being the first one to "discover" and "share" something of value to the team. And of course, they want access to collaboration tools in their companies that parallel the social experiences they have in their daily lives.

According to technology market research firm Forrester, forward-thinking organizations are already creating programs to identify, train and leverage key individuals—typically Millennials—to act as leaders in jumpstarting the process of integrating social technologies into their organizations.

One challenge is that Millennials are not enamored with traditional means of collaborating—scheduled telephone conference calls and in-person meetings. Instead they prefer real-time electronic communications and social collaboration. This will take some getting used to.

Still, companies stand to gain from a more collaborative environment: more meaningful interactions can spark innovation and great new ideas.

Millennials can help teach your company to embrace diversity. Diversity is well understood and accepted as a valuable hiring and organizational development strategy. But its scope continues to expand. Research shows that the target consumer for most global companies has undergone a dramatic transformation.

By way of example, in decades past the target consumer at American Express was the affluent, "frequent flyer," white American male. Today, there is no single target American Express consumer and as a group, American Express customers are increasingly diverse by almost every measure.

Here in the United States, women control 80% of household spending. When you add influence to direct buying power, the percentages for consumer goods and services such as vacations, cars, banking and computers rise above 90%. In addition the 50 million Hispanics now living in America also represent a potent new market for consumer purchases.

Equally profound are the large but immature markets that are growing in emerging nations. China has already surpassed Japan as the second-largest economy in the world. By 2020 economists predict that China will overtake the United States to claim the top spot.

I recently read an estimate from McKinsey & Company that a rapidly growing middle class in a dozen emerging nations has reached 2 billion people, and that their spending could reach $20 trillion by 2020—about twice the current consumption in the United States.

All of these new types of consumers represent an opportunity for American companies in international markets to gain sustainable advantages. But to do so, psychologically as well as operationally, winning companies will need a deep understanding of diversity, with many practices and current beliefs changing.

This is another area where Millennials can help. Unlike generations before them, Millennials are themselves ethnically and racially diverse. Many of them have already traveled extensively or studied abroad. They have friends all over the world and are comfortable with other cultures. They are open to living and working overseas.

In fact a recent study by PricewaterhouseCoopers revealed that 80% of Millennials would like to work abroad and 70% expect to use another language in their career.

That's great news for companies looking to tap emerging markets for growth.

Millennials can influence your company to be more socially responsible. When Millennials enter the workforce, they bring their attitudes about social responsibility with them. A recent Deloitte poll of 18-to-26-year olds revealed that 61% said they would prefer to work for an organization that offers volunteer opportunities. A MonsterTRAK poll found that 80% of Millennials would like a job that has a positive impact on the environment, and 92% would be more inclined to work for a company that's environmentally friendly.

This can be a good thing for your company: it has worked for IBM. In 2008, IBM launched its Corporate Service Corps to help provide Millennial and other IBMers with leadership development opportunities while satisfying their desire to solve problems for communities and organizations in need.

The program sends groups of 10 to 15 IBM employees from different countries and with different skills to four-week community-based volunteer assignments in emerging nations. Projects range from developing new technologies to support a burgeoning tourism market in Tanzania to creating a business plan for a non-profit focused on creative recycling of material to raise environmental awareness in the Philippines.

Since its launch, the IBM Corporate Service Corps has sent more than 1,400 of its employees in more than 120 teams to more than 20 countries around the world. The program expands to new locations each year. Participants have come from 50 different countries themselves.

At the program's founding, then IBM Chairman and CEO Sam Palmisano said that he fully expected the program to "make IBM a more competitive and successful business."

The program has become a model for others seeking ways to develop future leaders and establish themselves in emerging markets. IBM has helped a half-dozen other companies put together similar programs, including FedEx, John Deere and Dow Corning.

Even within IBM, demand for the program at all levels inspired its extension to executives at the company. In 2010, IBM launched the Executive Service Corps to help cities in emerging nations solve more complex problems.

Millennials can help you create an entrepreneurial culture. I opened this chapter with Mark Zuckerberg, the most well-known and successful Millennial entrepreneur so far. And even though there is just one Mark Zuckerberg and one Facebook, there are scores of other Millennial entrepreneurs who have achieved success in their own way and on their own scale.

Aaron Patzer founded Mint.com, a free online financial planning website, in 2007 out of frustration at how difficult it was to manage his personal finances online. He was 25. Two years later he sold the company to financial services giant Intuit for $170 million.

Betsy Johnson started her company, SwimZip, at the age of 27 after being diagnosed with skin cancer. The company sells stylish, zippered, UV 50 plus swimwear for babies, toddlers and children.

A co-founder of Pinterest—named by *Time* magazine as one of the 50 best sites of 2011—is 29-year-old Ben Silbermann. Launched in March 2010, less than two years later Pinterest was one of the top 10 largest social networks.

While some Millennials are hell-bent on starting their own companies, others do so because they believe that established companies cannot provide them with the creative, important, meaningful work they crave. In my view, this is a shame.

Think about it. Entrepreneurs do not feel they have the luxury of resting on their laurels. Every single day, they must put their reputations and their futures on the line. Every single day, they must beat the competition and deliver for their customers. If they don't, there is always someone else ready to step in and take their business away.

Sure, they have the advantage of independence—no one tells them what to do or how to do it. But no one is there to bail them out if they run into trouble either. Entrepreneurs must win every single day to survive, let alone thrive.

One reason is that for entrepreneurs, their businesses are not just what they do, but who they are. As a result, every success and every failure is personal—and the entrepreneurs I know take their results and failures very personally.

Entrepreneurs are focused on new things. They are driven to expand their base and identify new opportunities. To be successful, they know they must take risks—be more confident and resourceful and, at the same time, less afraid of what they don't know and more willing to seek advice when they need it.

Entrepreneurs also have a healthy paranoia about the competition. They know that threats can come from any direction at any time, and they stay alert to the possibility that if they don't take advantage of an opportunity, someone else will.

But entrepreneurs are not so focused on the competition that they forget their customers. In fact, just the opposite is true. Entrepreneurs stay incredibly close to their customers. They constantly listen, ask questions, anticipate their customers' needs, and work hard to exceed their customers' expectations. In other words, they think like their customers.

And finally, entrepreneurs are not afraid to change their strategies and plans—and quickly, if need be—to adapt to changing market conditions or a competitive threat or to capitalize on a new opportunity. This agility and nimbleness serves them well in a business climate where new competition can spring up without warning and new technologies can change the rules overnight.

Sounds like someone you'd want working for you, doesn't it? To me it also sounds a little bit like a

Millennial—especially one who has been coached in the realities of business by great mentors.

And it certainly reminds me of my dear friend and colleague, David Metcalf. A brilliant copywriter, David now runs his own advertising agency in New York City called Working Class, Inc. But in his younger days, he was trying to work his way up through the ranks of some of Manhattan's best advertising agencies. The problem was he had no patience for the meticulous process and careful communication required of agencies working for demanding clients. He freely admits that by the age of 40 he had been fired by three ad agencies for insubordination!

In truth, David was exceptionally committed to doing his very best work. He loved working for clients he believed in and who appreciated his talents. And he wanted work to be fun!

Ultimately, David had to step away from big agencies and form his own boutique ad shop to realize his dreams.

That raises my final question: can large companies create a culture in which Millennials' entrepreneurial drive can be channeled and flourish? I believe they can.

However—and make no mistake about this—an entrepreneurial culture is not for everyone. Some business leaders, for example, are content with more centralized, rigidly hierarchical organizational structures and a command-and-control management style. They would find a culture of entrepreneurship far too threatening to their authority.

And some managers working in large companies are quite fearful of the accountability that comes with the freedom to act like an entrepreneur. Some people prefer fixed job descriptions, little or no influence over important decisions and little control over their jobs. Some people prefer just putting in their time and going home at the end of the day. These people would not thrive in an entrepreneurial culture.

But these people usually are not Millennials. And so we are back to the question of how large companies can create an environment in which Millennials can contribute and feel professionally fulfilled. The answer begins at the top with leadership.

For starters, leaders must believe that people really are critical business assets…and not just costs to be minimized.

Leaders also must embrace new ways to empower people to achieve excellence…without fear of unleashing the power of people.

This is a great and necessary foundation. But there is more. Business leaders should ask themselves the following questions:

- Do you see yourself as a coach or a white knight self appointed to save everyone who works for you?

- How open are you in sharing information that could inspire members of your team, and the team as a whole, to perform better?

- How respectful are you of the different roles played by each member of your team and the unique skills they each bring to the team?

- Do you give your employees the authority to make decisions and act independently from you or do your own needs for control create dependency?

And finally, leaders must make sure that the entire organization adopts some basic practices that will help attract and engage Millennials. While there are many things you could do, in my view, there are six things you must do:

#1: Ensure your company's hiring model is open to hiring Millennials. Remember you actually want to hire people with their qualities, traits and values—not keep them out.

#2: Open up communication at all levels. Ask for input. Arm people with information. Without information, people cannot make responsible decisions. With it, it's hard not to. Millennials seek meaning in their work—being open, honest and transparent is a start.

#3: Make it personal. Did you know that 21% of workers don't know what their CEO looks like? That won't fly with Millennials.

#4: Give constant feedback. Communicate your expectations. Make it clear how each person contributes to the company, what their role is and how they will be evaluated. Let them know how they're doing—and what they could improve on. This is the kind of structure and coaching that Millennials need.

#5: Turn up the volume on trust. Give decision making to the experts—the people who are closest to the front lines of the business and your customers. Give them the confidence they need to act without fear.

#6: Celebrate your heroes. Spotlight and reward the behaviors and accomplishments of your employees. Millennials thrive on recognition for the contributions they make—and so does everyone else.

Bottom line, here is my message to you as a business leader in a time of great change: to keep up you must constantly be searching, evolving and finding new ways to do things. In Millennials you will find a generation with a passion for change and young people who would like nothing better than a chance to make a difference in your company. Let them. You won't regret it.

Who knows, 10 or 15 years from now, you might even end up working for one.

BRANDS
IN A DIGITAL WORLD

How has digital technology changed consumer expectations?

What is the new consumer journey
and where do brands fit in?

Technology for business has advanced at an amazing rate over the past few decades, and I have certainly benefited from it during my 50-year career. But even someone my age knows that for the last 10 years the real action has been in technology for consumers. It's been on fire with innovation.

Look around. We have near-instantaneous and unlimited access to communications, information and interaction through the Internet, social media and mobile technologies. Broadband Internet access gives us 24/7 high-speed connectivity. Camera-equipped smartphones and tablets with razor-sharp screen quality provide us with access to rich content and interesting applications.

And while my younger co-workers, grandchildren, and the teenage children of co-workers and my staff are perfectly at home in this digital world, to me these are astonishing innovations that enrich nearly every aspect of our daily lives.

To understand my perspective, remember that I was in my 20s in the 1950s. Back then televisions and copy machines qualified as new technologies. Rocket science was the cool new industry. Our knowledge of computers was based on ENIAC—essentially a giant calculator made out of 18,000 vacuum tubes that was capable of multiplying numbers rapidly and not much more. It would be 25 years before the first personal computer was introduced.

So you can see that for me today's consumer technologies are nothing less than miraculous.

In particular, mobile technologies are compelling—convenient, engaging, fun. It's no surprise that people have embraced them completely without looking back.

I have to keep reminding myself that the mobile revolution is relatively new—the first widely available smartphone was introduced in 2001 and the first successful tablet computer in 2010—because the numbers already tell an unprecedented story of consumer adoption.

- There are more than 6 billion mobile phone subscriptions in the world, including more than 950 million smartphone subscriptions. 83% of U.S. adults own a cell phone and of those, 42% own smartphones.

- 38 million tablet computers will be sold to U.S. consumers in 2012, surpassing sales of laptop computers for the first time, which will reach 31 million units.

- Tablet sales already dwarf those of desktop PCs—just 19 million desktop units were sold in 2011. That number will drop to just over 18 million units in 2012.

As someone who has spent the better part of his career marketing consumer brands, it's clear to me that mobile devices in particular have changed the way consumers do just about everything—work, play, learn, shop and connect with friends and family.

As I write this in July 2012:

- Every day, consumers conduct billions of searches on popular search engines and social networking sites. They search for information on everything—from bankruptcy to basketball, marriage to mortgage calculators. They search for news and analysis—how does the U.S. Supreme Court ruling on the health care reform law affect uninsured children? Why did Katie Holmes divorce Tom Cruise? They search for people they went to high school with.

- 500 or so legitimate music services around the world offer more than 20 million songs. Sometimes consumers buy them and download them on to their computers or mobile devices. Sometimes they just rent them and have them streamed.

▶ The Apple App Store now has about 675,000 "active" apps—apps that people are still downloading and using every day. That number includes about 120,000 games and 65,000 books. Consumers download items from the App Store at the rate of about 45 million per day.

▶ The number of registered users of Facebook has reached and quickly passed 950 million. Facebook accounts for 1 of every 5 pages viewed on the web. Consumers upload more than 250 million photos every day.

▶ Twitter users now send more than 400 million tweets a day. When Steve Jobs died 6,000 tweets per second were sent at their peak. A television airing in Japan of the classic Japanese Anime movie *Castle in the Sky* set an all-time tweets-per-second record of more than 25,000.

▶ 800 million unique users visit YouTube each month and watch 4 billion videos every day. Five hundred years worth of YouTube videos are watched every day on Facebook.

- More than 80% of Millennials (also known as Generation Y)—the largest consumer group in history—are influenced by user-generated content (reviews, ratings, tips) when considering a purchase. 51% rate the aggregated opinions of strangers as more important than those of their friends and family.

- 70% of the 245 million Americans who go online will buy something online this year.

Digital technology changes everything for everyone

The ubiquity of the Internet, social media and mobile devices has had a profound affect on consumers' daily lives. And as a result, its impact on businesses that serve consumers has been no less seismic.

I have certainly observed how it has changed American Express. Over the past five years, digital technology has transformed how the company engages with consumers, merchants and partners.

This is no accident: American Express was determined to be at the forefront of the digital revolution.

It started at the top, with CEO Ken Chenault establishing the critical objective of "transforming all of our

businesses for the digital marketplace." It now has fil-
tered down and out to every corner of the company. Its
influence can be seen everywhere.

As Senior Advisor to Ken Chenault, I sit in on what
are called "shirt-sleeve sessions," which are meetings of
executives at the company where the company's top
initiatives are discussed and dissected. Often running
these meetings are the senior leaders and architects of
the American Express digital-social-mobile strategy and
many of the people who make it work day to day.

I have listened with fascination and admiration over
the past five years as yet another chapter in the continu-
ous renewal of American Express has been written.

I have more to say about American Express and how
it has reinvented its brand for the digital world. I will
do so later in this chapter. But first I want to talk about
the impact digital technology has had on business
in general.

Exciting new industries and companies are spring-
ing up to serve newly empowered social-mobile consumers. We all know about Facebook and Twitter.
There are many other companies whose offerings
and business models would not be possible without
digital technology:

- Hulu offers on-demand television and movies for free with an ad-supported model and also through subscriptions.

- Spotify, a digital media company, brings us legal on-demand access to music and is an alternative to iTunes.

- Groupon offers a "daily online deal" on things to do, eat, see and buy in a particular city—a certain number of people must sign up for the deal for it to be delivered.

- Pinterest, described as a "virtual pinboard," lets us share ideas and plan weddings, decorate our homes and organize such things as recipe and photo collections.

Digital technology hasn't been kind to every business. The publishing industry is barely recognizable today—a victim, so to speak, of user-generated content, citizen journalists and the self-publishing trend.

For example, newspaper publishers have lost $27 billion in print advertising revenues since 2005 while gaining just $1.2 billion in new revenue from their digital ventures.

Travel agencies, bookstores and video rental companies have not fared any better.

And some iconic brands of 20th century America have not survived:

- Tower Records, which started in California in the 1960s and dominated music retailing, went bankrupt and closed its stores in 2006—displaced by online music downloads.

- Eastman Kodak, the 131-year-old company that pioneered the film industry, filed for bankruptcy protection in January 2012 after years of failing to adapt to digital film technology.

- After 244 years, Encyclopedia Britannica stopped publishing its printed multi-volume book sets in March 2012, although it remains an online information resource.

Brands in the digital world

The concept of brands and brand marketing originated in the 19th century when mass-production techniques for a variety of basic household products resulted in more choice and consistent quality at a lower cost. But it wasn't until the 1960s that professional brand marketing flourished.

In those days—and for the better part of two decades—a perfect strategy for persuading consumers to trust and buy a product or service was to tightly control the brand and the consumer experience of it.

Those days are gone.

Instead, today's consumers want to engage, participate and influence. They want to be heard, understood and acknowledged. They want two-way conversations not one-way communications. And they are empowered in these desires by technology that helps them make faster, smarter, more informed buying decisions.

All of this has resulted in a new consumer journey—the path consumers take while making the decision to purchase one brand over another.

Most marketers are familiar with the "funnel" model of the consumer purchase decision and the concept of "touch points"—specific moments in time when consumers' purchase decisions can be influenced.

In the funnel purchase model consumers start with a large number of potential brands in mind, and then can be moved by marketing through a linear series of steps. Along the way they systematically narrow down the brands they are considering until they purchase one.

Research done in 2009 by McKinsey & Company examined the purchase decisions of nearly 20,000 consumers across five industries and three continents. The results provide an instructive view of how—and how much—digital technology has changed the consumer journey.

Among McKinsey's findings were the following:

- ▶ The consumer journey is more circular than linear, with phases rather than steps. McKinsey identified and named four phases: initial consideration; active evaluation or research; closure, when purchases are made; and post-purchase, when consumers experience the products and services they have bought.

- ▶ Bombarded with too many messages and overwhelmed by too many choices, rather than starting with a large number of brands consumers actually start with a relatively small number. However, during the evaluation phase, they are just as likely to expand the number of brands they are considering as they are to reduce them.

- ▶ Consumers empowered by technology actively "pull" information that draws them closer to purchase twice as often as they allow themselves to be "pushed" by marketers.

For brands and their marketers, the implications of the McKinsey research are profound:

● Digital technology dramatically changes the journey that consumers take—starting with first becoming aware of a brand to making the decision to purchase.

● Instead of being orderly, planned and largely controlled by the brand, the new consumer journey is fueled by digital touch points that consumers encounter along the way.

● Marketers can still neatly plan some of these digital touch points. But increasingly consumers are having serendipitous interactions with brands on the Internet, social media networks and in the physical world augmented by digital experiences.

● While traditional marketing remains important, rather than trying to control the consumer journey, marketers must align with the consumer journey to influence the purchase decision. In other words, rather than bringing consumers to brands, brands must be where consumers are.

One of the most fascinating examples I've seen of marketing aligned with the new consumer journey is a free mobile app called Price Check from Amazon. Here's how it works.

You're shopping at a retail store and you see an item you want to purchase. You wonder if you can get that same item for a better price somewhere else. Using the Price Check app on your smartphone, you can scan the product's barcode, take a picture of the product, say the product's name or type it in.

With your smartphone's location service switched on—which enables the phone to pinpoint your exact GPS location—you press the Submit Price button. Price Check then presents you with prices for that item from offline retailers close to your location and from online retailers, including Amazon.

If you like Amazon's price, you can place the item in the app's shopping cart and buy it on the spot. You also have the option of buying it any time over the next 24 hours.

In short, while you are physically in a retail store about to make a purchase, Amazon can take the sale away from that retailer without the retailer even knowing it!

The benefit to you as a consumer is obvious— you get a valuable price comparison shopping service for free and possibly the best price for an item you want to buy.

As for Amazon, the company gets more business from you, of course. But Amazon also gets competitive pricing information that it can use to price its own products—collected by you, the consumer, for Amazon at little or no cost to Amazon.

This is a win-win for both you and Amazon—but not so much for the retailer that lost your business.

The retail industry calls what Price Check enables "showrooming"—the practice of coming into a store to see a product in person, but then purchasing it from an online retailer, usually at a lower price. Of course, retailers don't like it at all.

Retail giants such as Walmart, Target and Best Buy are fighting back with apps and mobile shopping tools of their own. They're also placing computers and kiosks inside their stores that let consumers check prices and get more information about the product in case they don't have their mobile phones with them.

However, unlike the Amazon app—which presents prices from many sources, and takes its chances that Amazon will win enough new business from you to make the app worthwhile—tools from these other retailers bring consumers right back to their own websites.

Target is apparently taking its response to Amazon one step further. Earlier this year, the chain was rumored to have asked its vendors to provide it with more unique merchandise, reasoning that if the product is not available anywhere else, showrooming is not possible.

The good news is that in all of these scenarios, consumers win—with more choice, more valuable shopping services and better prices.

Established brands, savvy marketers

Amazon Price Check is a small but powerful illustration of how digital touch points can be aligned to interact with consumers, changing forever how they discover, consider, select and purchase. But Amazon was "born digital," and so perhaps we should expect nothing less.

There are, however, great examples of traditional companies and brands that have also mastered customer engagement in the digital world.

Remember back in 2010 when Old Spice—a line of men's grooming products first introduced in the 1930s—created a new television ad campaign? It starred a very funny football player turned actor, Isaiah Mustafa.

The first ad—"The Man Your Man Could Smell Like"—featured Mustafa speaking rapidly to women, presenting one fantasy scenario after another. It first aired during the Super Bowl. Videos of the ads on a sponsored YouTube channel went viral.

Buoyed by success, in the summer of 2010, Old Spice launched one of the fastest growing online video campaigns ever. Called "Old Spice Responses," the campaign first seeded various social media sites with an invitation to ask questions of Mustafa.

Then the campaign did something very bold and even by today's standards, remarkable.

All of the people who contributed interesting questions, or were high profile people on social networks, were responded to directly and by name in short, funny videos—more than 180 in all—that appeared on the Old Spice sponsored channel on YouTube. And here's the kicker: these response videos were written, produced and delivered over a time period of 24 hours.

The campaign was widely successful. The Old Spice
YouTube channel became the number one viewed
sponsored channel on YouTube with 236 million
views. The brand gained 80,000 Twitter followers in
two days. The personalized videos increased Facebook
interaction by 800%. Traffic on the oldspice.com website grew by 300%.

Sales of Old Spice more than doubled in 30 days.

Be true to your brand

Old Spice is a fantastic example of an established brand
reinventing itself for social media.

But I do want to be clear about one thing. When I
talk about brands reinventing themselves in the digital
world, I do not mean they changed what their brands
stand for, their brand promise or their core values.

In fact, the successful brands have done just the opposite. That's because in a digital world—where brands
matter but authenticity, honesty and transparency rule
the day—brands must stay true to themselves. Brands
that fail or sell out pay the price. Here's an example:

In 2009, PepsiCo released an iPhone app to promote
its AMP drink, which is promoted as an energy drink

for men in all aspects of their lives, not just in their athletic pursuits. The app was called "AMP Up Before You Score" and was designed to help men seduce women.

I'm not joking.

Categorizing women into 24 different types—Bookworm, Cougar, Women's Studies Major—the app offered pick up lines that each type would supposedly find appealing. Worse, the app offered a "brag" feature that encouraged men to include the name, date and details of both successful and failed encounters.

While the app may not have violated the brand values of AMP, it certainly was not what most consumers have come to expect from PepsiCo. CEO Indra Nooyi has often been quoted saying she wants PepsiCo to be "a model of how to conduct business in the modern world" and "part of the solution, not the cause of some of society's biggest social problems."

Predictably, the app outraged both women and men and was excoriated by the media. PepsiCo quickly removed the app and offered a public apology.

Lesson learned.

More than the sum of its parts

While there are many examples of social media "fails" among established brands reinventing themselves for the digital world—campaigns that offend or simply fall flat—there are an increasing number who are getting it right. Whole Foods is one of them.

Whole Foods is an established company that has embraced social media more than most and had more success than most. The organic grocery chain was founded in 1980 and today has nearly 300 locations in North America and the United Kingdom.

What's especially fascinating about Whole Foods as a social media success story is this. In the early days of its campaign Whole Foods CEO John Mackey was the central figure in an online scandal that illustrates just how carefully companies must navigate social media— and how quickly a company can damage its reputation with missteps.

In early 2007, Whole Foods made an offer to acquire Wild Oats Markets, a small rival in the natural foods business. In early June 2007 the Federal Trade Commission (FTC) filed a lawsuit attempting to block the purchase on anti-trust grounds.

Whole Foods responded to the lawsuit both in the court of law and the court of public opinion. In addition to issuing seven press releases on the topic over the first 30 days, Mackey tackled the lawsuit's premise in his personal blog, which he had started in 2005 and that was hosted on the Whole Food's website.

In a series of strident defenses and arguments, Mackey attacked and refuted the FTC's position. One of his consistent themes was his intention for every aspect of the acquisition to be completely transparent to Whole Foods' stakeholders and the public.

Then in mid-July, the *Wall Street Journal* broke the story that among the FTC's allegations was that for eight years Mackey had posted disparaging comments about Wild Oats on an Internet financial forum— and that he had done so using a pseudonym that masked his identity.

Both Mackey and the company admitted the allegations were true. But they vigorously defended Mackey's actions, eventually settling on the position that Mackey was speaking for himself in the financial forum and not for the company.

Within a few days, however, both the FTC and the Whole Foods Board of Directors launched formal inquiries to determine whether anything Mackey had done was illegal. Mackey put his blog on hold.

The acquisition was approved in August 2007 but the formal inquiries into Mackey's actions continued until May 2008, when both the FTC and his Board cleared him of any wrongdoing. Mackey resumed blogging. His first post was a 2,000-word defense of his anonymous postings.

What Mackey did was judged "not illegal," but many believed it showed an appalling lack of ethics and judgment. Although Mackey and Whole Foods had some vocal supporters, many members of the press, bloggers and Whole Foods' own customers soundly criticized the company for what was perceived as a breach of trust.

Shareholders were not very happy either, and expressed their displeasure in the company's stock price. Consensus was that Mackey had certainly violated unwritten rules about how corporations are expected to behave on the Internet. Whole Foods was considered complicit for its blind defense of its CEO.

Mackey remained unapologetic—and over the last four years has continued to express his often-controversial opinions in his personal blog.

Whole Foods suffered reputation damage during this period and certainly lost the confidence of some of its shareholders and customers forever. But the company recovered and today is frequently held up as model of social media success.

How could Whole Foods have achieved redemption so quickly? In part through a social media strategy built on the following fundamental principles:

- Whole Foods maintains its position that what John Mackey writes in his personal blog does not necessarily reflect the opinions of the company.

Every other aspect of the company's social media strategy focuses on customers and communities and shies away from controversy.

- Whole Foods understands its different types of customers, prizes interacting with them and provides each type with content tailored to their interests.

Content in the company's social channels ranges from recipes to articles about sustainable foods to garden tips and current food industry news. Every store has a Facebook page and so a large percentage of Whole Foods' social content is local.

● Whole Foods uses a variety of social channels to engage with its different types of customers. Each channel has its primary goal—but all of the channels are linked at the level of positioning and strategy.

Whole Foods' company blog (which is separate from Mackey's personal blog) is the hub of its social media strategy. It is rich with content of its own, but includes links to all of its other social channels.

Facebook is used to engage new customers and re-engage with existing customers. Twitter is used primarily as a customer service tool. The company's YouTube channel has educational and how-to videos as well as stories. Pinterest is used to engage customers in food and home projects. The Whole Foods iPhone app helps customers search for recipes and locate stores.

● Whole Foods emphasizes information, education and valuable content over hard selling.

While Whole Foods makes information about store discounts, bargains and coupons available to its customers, the company stresses engagement, interaction and feedback over selling in its content.

- Whole Foods creates new content daily so there is always something fresh, new and interesting.

In addition to rich content generated by Whole Foods, all of its social channels welcome comments, feedback and user-generated content.

- Whole Foods stays true to its brand across all social channels.

Whole Foods' motto is "Whole Foods, Whole People, Whole Planet." As a natural and organic food company, there are certain types of foods or ingredients it will not sell. It emphasizes healthy products and foods. It strives to feature sustainable food selections. Whether you are walking up and down the aisles of a Whole Foods store or visiting one of its many social channels, these values shine through.

Of all the things Whole Foods does right in social media, it is perhaps most respected for its integration of social channels. With its company blog serving as the hub, Facebook, Twitter, YouTube, and all of its other social channels support and extend the company's website, providing a dynamic and engaging social media presence everywhere its customers go.

Lasting relationships, exchanges of value

Earlier in this chapter, I promised to talk more about how American Express has embraced social-mobile media.

As you know, American Express was founded more than 160 years ago, and today is a leader in financial services and one of the world's most respected service brands. I spent the majority of my professional life helping ensure its strength and longevity. The company and the brand hold a special place in my mind and heart.

American Express marketing has always received high marks for its intelligence, artistic creativity and its effectiveness at building lasting relationships. Everything the company does is aimed at engaging customers, merchants and partners in long-term relationships that create value.

For all of these reasons, I am proud to add American Express to the list of established companies getting it right in the digital world.

In case you think I am too biased, earlier this year, *Fast Company* magazine named American Express to its top 10 in social media list for 2012. The designation recognized the company's practice of "iterating like a startup" and innovations such as Serve, a mobile platform that lets people send and store money without going through a bank.

Also this year, research firm Corporate Insight named American Express as the financial services firm that best uses social media. Noting that American Express was a pioneer in social media—in 2007 the company launched OPEN Forum, an online resource and social networking hub for small businesses—the firm noted that the company "manages to use more social media channels more effectively than any other [financial services] firm."

In fact American Express actively engages consumers through Facebook, Twitter, YouTube, LinkedIn and Foursquare. On Facebook, American Express features images and photos of members and partners, and builds a following with exclusive offers to people who "like" the page, and emphasizes entertainment as much as information.

American Express uses Twitter to distribute content and answer questions from consumers. In recent years, Twitter has become a key component of the company's new customer service strategy, which has been revamped to stress relationships instead of transactions.

An American Express branded YouTube channel showcases videos created expressly for a YouTube audience as well as repurposed videos from traditional media such as television.

American Express uses LinkedIn to reach a network of 150 million high-income and high-net-worth professionals, many of whom are ideal target consumers for American Express.

American Express uses the location-based technologies of Foursquare—a free app that lets people "check in" to places they visit and share and save information with them—to provide incentives for merchants and consumers to use the American Express Card.

Among the fundamental principles of all American Express social-mobile activities are the following: the company tries to be everywhere its members and partners are; it puts them first; and it emphasizes building lasting relationships based on exchanges of value.

Of the many social-mobile activities American Express uses to engage consumers, two stand out: "Sync" and "Small Business Saturday."

Sync is an innovative social offering for consumers made possible by American Express and its merchants working together as partners through social channels.

After linking an American Express Card to one of their social media accounts, Cardholders can access deals from merchants they like—companies such as Whole Foods, 1-800-Flowers.com, FedEx Office, Virgin America and Zappos. No coupon is necessary—just the link and a qualifying purchase.

American Express launched Sync with Foursquare in June 2011 and a month later added Facebook. On Facebook, once a card has been linked, consumers can access deals simply by "liking" a brand.

Sync was an evolving success story until this past spring, when American Express added Twitter to the list of social channels supporting the program and launched the new partnership at South-by-Southwest (SXSW) 2012—an annual music, film, interactive conference and festival held in Austin, Texas. The combination was explosive.

SXSW began 25 years ago as a small music festival for emerging bands—it is credited with helping launch the careers of performers such as Amy Winehouse, The White Stripes and Norah Jones—and is now hugely popular. Small bands still perform, but in recent years SXSW has attracted major artists as headliners, including Lil Wayne and Kanye West. Bruce Springsteen was this year's keynote speaker.

By many accounts, American Express "stole the show" at SXSW when it launched Sync for Twitter and offered tickets to a Jay-Z concert to attendees who completed a sync of an American Express Card to Twitter. Of course the venue and the star power of Jay-Z had a lot to do with it. But Twitter seems tailor made for an offering like Sync—iPhone and Android smartphone users are 60% of all Twitter users.

To take advantage of Sync on Twitter, Cardmembers simply sync an eligible card to Twitter and then tweet a hashtag—a word or phrase with the # symbol in front of it that Twitter uses to organize topics by groups—specific to the special offer. The offer is automatically loaded directly onto the synced card and once it is used, the savings from the deal are automatically credited to the Cardmember's statement.

In my view, Sync on Twitter is a brilliant example of a social offering that engages consumers where they like to be and benefits all parties—consumers, merchants, Twitter and American Express.

Another innovative American Express offering enabled by social channels is Small Business Saturday, a national initiative begun in 2010 to level the playing field for small businesses during the holiday shopping season. Small Business Saturday is as much a movement as it is a marketing program. It encourages consumers to shop at their favorite local businesses on the Saturday between Black Friday and Cyber Monday—shopping days that have been largely the domain of big-box and online retailers.

In 2011, Small Business Saturday worked like this. Through its OPEN small business network, American Express offered small business tools, promotional materials and incentives for consumers who shop locally. The materials available on OPEN were promoted through a special Small Business Saturday Facebook page and an @ShopSmall Twitter account. Small business owners also were offered free Facebook advertising, paid for by American Express.

For consumers, American Express offered a $25 statement credit for anyone who registered a card and then spent at least $25 at a local business on Small Business Saturday—which hundreds of thousands of consumers did.

While American Express made significant investments of its own, the company's merchant and other partners helped as well by offering gift cards and running their own Small Business Saturday promotional campaigns.

At a time in our economy when all businesses are suffering—and especially small businesses—the program quickly gained national attention from elected officials. President Obama tweeted his support of the program using the #smallbusinesssaturday hashtag.

By social media marketing measures, Small Business Saturday 2012 was a huge success. More than 2.7 million people "liked" the Small Business Saturday Facebook page. Close to 195 million tweets were sent in support of the program during the month of November. Awareness of the program rose from 37% in 2010 to 65% in 2011.

Most important an estimated 103 million Americans shopped at small businesses on Small Business Saturday and American Express transactions among small business merchants increased by 23%. While more sales at small businesses certainly benefited American Express, they helped small businesses even more.

Netting it out

Despite the success of Old Spice, Whole Foods, American Express and others, many established brands still struggle with how to reinvent themselves in the digital world. Believe me—as someone not "born digital"—I completely understand.

For as the companies highlighted in this chapter demonstrate, attracting consumers to a brand today takes vastly different marketing strategies than have worked in the past.

For starters, brands today must be agile and strive to encounter instead of control consumers in the digital world. This involves creating some of their own digital touch points and exploiting others that already exist.

Brands also must understand each of their customer types and visualize how they appear to each type of consumer in various social channels such as Facebook, Twitter and YouTube. In particular they must learn to recognize how consumers form emotional attachments with brands in these channels and create engaging content and activities that help foster those bonds.

At the same time, brands must look at how channels integrate and work together as well as how they stand alone. This requires a thoughtful and comprehensive strategy.

All along the way, brands must constantly strive to gain new insights into the triggers and behaviors that affect the twists and turns of the new consumer journey—and recognize that these can change quickly with the rise and fall of the popularity of different social channels.

This is already a long list. But there are a few more things I've learned from my colleagues at American Express and from my own research that companies with established brands should consider as they brave this new world.

> ● There is not now and never will be one way to succeed in the digital world.

Successful companies don't spend all of their time searching for best practices, templates or step-by-step instructions on how to engage consumers through social channels. They combine the very best thinking of those who know the brand and its values, its customers and social media. And they create their own experiences. When they fail, they fail fast and move on. When they succeed, they don't assume that the same things will work next time.

> ● Social media is about people, not channels.

With all the attention being paid to Facebook and Twitter—and the other social channels of the moment—

it's easy to forget that consumers are people who are influenced by other people and the decisions they make are as often emotional as rational. Companies too often make the mistake of thinking they need a Twitter strategy instead of a strategy for engaging with consumers through social channels. Social media works best when you start with who your consumers are and what they need—and then find and use all the channels that can help influence their journey.

● Social media needs to serve a purpose.

As many companies now know, simply saying "Follow us on Twitter!" or "Like us on Facebook!" is not an effective strategy for engaging consumers. Instead consumers need a compelling reason to engage with a brand—they must see clearly that there is a purpose behind the interaction that benefits them or a cause they care about.

● Lasting relationships with consumers are just as difficult to create in social media as in the real world.

Sometimes it is easy to think that Facebook "likes," Twitter "follows," and YouTube "views" equal success. But lasting relationships with your consumers are created with time, trust and exchanges of value—not with expressions of the moment that are easy to do and just as easy to forget.

❯ Social media is not a direct marketing channel.

Many established companies in particular are uncomfortable with social media because it is difficult to measure. While social media measurement techniques are evolving along with the channels themselves, there will always be an element of uncertainty and unpredictability to interactions with consumers. Don't try to treat social media like you might traditional marketing strategies.

If you do, you will undermine the very things that build brands and relationships through these amazing new channels.

AFTERWORD

I hope you have found my perspectives on the power of reinvention provocative and useful. From leadership in the new normal to talent in the 21st century to brands in a digital world, I have posed, and tried to answer, some essential questions that may help you drive progress.

I would like to leave you with a few closing thoughts on these topics, but first there is one more thing I'd like to address: the decline of ethical standards in American business.

Call to action

Recent polls of the American public show that animosity toward big business and especially Wall Street is at its highest level in 40 years. With home foreclosures, business and personal bankruptcies, and unemployment at unacceptably high levels, I don't have to tell you why.

More important than who is to blame is looking at what is actually happening across the broad ethical landscape of American business. The short answer to the current state of business ethics is that it is a mixed bag.

Research conducted in 2011 and reported in January 2012 by the Ethics Resource Center (ERC), America's oldest nonprofit devoted to independent research and the advancement of high ethical standards in public and private institutions, revealed the following:

- Over the previous two years, 45% of U.S. employees had observed a violation of the law or ethics standards at their places of employment.

- Reporting of wrongdoing was at an all-time high—65%—but so too was retaliation against whistleblowers: more than one in five employees who reported misconduct said they experienced some sort of retaliation.

- Ethics cultures in business are at their weakest point since 2000—the percentage of businesses with weak cultures is 42%, a seven-percentage point increase over 2009, when the most recent previous ERC survey was conducted.

But here is something interesting—and dismaying, in my view: companies that earn the most revenue work hard to build strong ethics programs and cultures, but face unique pressures that drive up the level of misconduct in their workplaces.

This was a key finding of the ERC's first-ever national business ethics survey of nearly 2,000 workers at Fortune 500 companies, conducted between June 7 and June 13, 2012. Consistent with the mixed findings of surveys of workers at all businesses, misconduct is higher in Fortune 500 companies and so is reporting —and retaliation.

- ○ 52% of employees of Fortune 500 companies reported having observed misconduct in their companies, compared with 45% at all companies.

- ○ 74% said they reported the misconduct in their companies, compared with 65% in all companies.

- ○ 25% who reported misconduct said they experienced retaliation, compared with one in five at all companies.

Equally important to understanding the current state of business ethics is looking ahead to how business can rebuild the trust and confidence of customers and other stakeholders that is necessary for success.

Given that Fortune 500 companies are the leaders in our economy, I would also like to think of them as leaders and role models in business ethics. And I am very proud to say that American Express is highly regarded for its ethical standards and conduct.

For five years running, American Express has been named one of the "World's Most Ethical Companies" by Ethisphere Institute, an international think tank focused on global business ethics and compliance. American Express is one of just four companies—the others being Starbucks, GE and Target—that have made the list all five years that Ethisphere has been ranking companies.

But establishing high ethical standards and living up to them on a daily basis are two different things. First, businesses must make decisions based on ethical guiding principles—instead of letting the decisions that are made drive their principles. This is a given, but it bears repeating.

Beyond that, businesses must periodically rethink and redefine their roles within society. At a time when confidence in business is so low, for example, leaders could make a larger and deeper commitment to ethics and transparency. And frankly, that is what is required in a world in which the Internet has shifted power away from corporations to consumers.

Just ask Barclays.

In June 2012 Barclays introduced a fictional character named Dan on its Facebook page. Dan, a hapless consumer that Barclays condescendingly referred to as "useless" in matters of budgeting, made his debut the day before Barclays was slapped with a $450 million fine for its role in manipulating the interest rate known as LIBOR. The LIBOR rate affects everything from credit card rates and mortgages to student loans.

It didn't take long for Barclays customers to co-opt Dan and turn him around as a tool to ridicule the bank. Here is one typical post about Dan from Barclays, followed by comments from customers:

Barclays: "Dan's an HR manager and spends £5 a day on lunch. That's about £100 a month; enough to buy a ticket to the vintage car festival he really wants to go to in August. Bringing food from home for a couple of months would mean a more memorable end to the summer. So come on Dan, get to making those sandwiches and book those festival tickets."

Customer: "Dan's festival fund is suddenly wiped out by an inexplicable hike in his mortgage rate."

Customer: "I don't care about 'Dan'. Dan is a HR Manager and likes vintage car festivals. On top of that, he seems to be getting financial advice from Barclays bank. The man's an idiot."

Another hard lesson learned.

And another good reason for a call to action to American business: isn't it time we ushered in a new era of business ethics?

Leadership

In closing, I'd like to offer the following additional thoughts on my three main areas of focus in this book: the reinvention of leadership, talent and brands.

On leadership, I want to acknowledge that even with the desire and a framework for reinvention, it's not an easy path. Changing old habits and patterns is always hard, and when we run into obstacles, it's tempting to fall back into old ways or scale back on our grand plans and aim for more modest goals.

The problem with taking small steps forward and making a few tweaks here and there is that the results often fall short of the bold actions that are necessary for reinvention. Therefore, boldness must be hardwired into strategy. We must be able to envision the future; the journey must be equally clear; we must innovate everywhere; and we must act with appropriate speed.

So I caution you about the dangers of acting incrementally, and instead encourage you to take the calculated risks necessary to move your business forward in different and new directions.

I also offer you the following questions as touchstones—things to ask yourselves every day—because you must be agents of change:

- ▶ "Is what I am doing enough?"

- ▶ "Does it meet the urgency of our challenge?"

- ▶ "If not, what am I doing about it?"

Talent

Turning next to talent, I would like to tell you a true story about my friend, David Ogilvy. I have already referenced him in this book—as you know, he was a brilliant advertising man and founder of one of the world's largest advertising agencies.

What you may not know is that David did not enter the profession he revolutionized until he was 38 years old. Born in England in 1911, he studied at Oxford but never graduated. After leaving Oxford, he worked in Paris in the kitchen of the Hotel Majestic, return-ing later to England to sell cooking stoves door to door.

In 1938, David immigrated to the United States, where he went to work for Gallup, the foremost consumer opinion research firm. During World War II, he worked with the Intelligence Service at the British Embassy in Washington. After the war, he bought a farm in Pennsylvania and lived among the Amish. In 1948, David founded the advertising agency that became Ogilvy & Mather.

Thirty-three years later, David sent the following memo to one of his partners:

> *Will Any Agency Hire This Man?*
>
> *He is 38, and unemployed. He dropped out of college. He has been a cook, a salesman, a diplomatist and a farmer. He knows noth-ing about marketing and has never written any copy. He professes to be interested in advertising as a career (at the age of 38!) and is ready to go to work for $5,000 a year.*
>
> *I doubt if any American agency will hire him.*

> *However, a London agency did hire him. Three years later he became the most famous copywriter in the world, and in due course built the tenth biggest agency in the world.*
>
> *The moral: It sometimes pays an agency to be imaginative and unorthodox in hiring.*

I'm sure the message is clear. As any CEO worth his or her salt will tell you, talent is the single most important driver of business success—and finding the right people is always a challenge.

Whether we are talking about women in leadership positions, veterans returning from the Middle East wars, Millennials or any other category of individuals that might be unfamiliar to us, the key to building a 21st century workforce is to be inclusive and reach out to people of all generations and all backgrounds with an open mind.

Equally important once you have them in your organization, your task is to present them with an environment and opportunities that give them the same potential to succeed as anyone else, but in their own unique ways.

Brands

On brands, I'd like to leave you with the following, somewhat sobering, reality. Perhaps the biggest impact of digital technology is this: speed matters like never before, and the new standard for engaging and interacting with consumers is real time, not your time. That means that before you even get started, you're too late!

Here is one way to think about solving this problem. Do you know how long it takes to stop a supertanker? The longest manmade vehicles in the world, supertankers have enormous inertia. Exact results vary depending on the size and weight of each ship, but a crash stop maneuver—meaning from "full ahead" to "full reverse"—can stop a fully loaded supertanker in a little less than two miles and in about 14 minutes.

Now in some situations this might be fast enough. But if you're a supertanker captain and you've just spotted a small craft dead ahead…well, you can only imagine the catastrophe that awaits.

So the only solution when it comes to your brand, social media and the real-time nature of the web, is to organize your company like a high-speed, open-ocean racing boat rather than a supertanker. Plan to act quickly and learn to anticipate rather than waiting for the vulnerable small craft to enter your line of sight to react.

This requires mapping and understanding your own consumer journey in advance, developing a strategy that will work across all social channels and creating a story whose individual elements can be told anywhere at anytime.

And then you must empower your employees to act with great speed and independence—to go with the flow of consumers and not try to throttle them back to your own more comfortable pace.

Finally, my last word on the power of reinvention is this: as complex and uncertain as today's world might seem, it is the perfect time to think about renewal and act on reinvention.

And if setbacks occur—or your own strong emotions get in the way—remember this:

The key is to just keep going.

Brands

Companies

Topics

ABOUT THE AUTHOR

Aldo Papone has been a central figure at American Express for nearly 40 years. While playing operational and advisory roles within the company, he consulted with many other companies on brand management and advertising, including Xerox Corporation for 13 years. He also served on numerous Boards of Directors for both corporations and non-profit organizations. Currently he is Co-Chair of the Board of Trustees of the Hospital for Special Surgery in New York City.

Mr. Papone was born and educated in Europe and came to America as a young man, beginning his career with Macy's in 1956. In 1974 he joined American Express and in 1989 he was elected Chairman and CEO of American Express

Travel Related Services. He is currently a Senior Advisor to American Express.

A popular speaker, Mr. Papone focuses on leadership, branding and marketing issues. In 2005, he authored The Power of the Obvious: Notes from 50 Years in Corporate America. *Earlier, he was an active spokesperson for the tourism and consumer credit industries, speaking frequently in the United States and abroad, and testifying many times before Congressional committees.*

Mr. Papone has wide-ranging cultural interests but is especially devoted to 19th century opera. He and his wife Sandra live in Greenwich, Connecticut. They have a daughter and two grandchildren.